Even MORE

by Trudie Hughes

Acknowledgments

My special thanks to:

Joyce Mottern of St. Louis for sharing her scrap quilt design, Road to St. Louis;

Joan Padgett and Lynette Chiles of Tomorrow's Heirlooms for letting me use their design, Shortcut to School;

Ruth Hartung of Imagine That for sharing her design, Danish Hearts;

Donna Eines for her adaptation of the Burgoyne Surrounded border;

Nancy and Dan Martin who believed in me;

The staff of Patched Works, who gave me the time to work on my book;

And last, but not least, to David Hughes, who let his mom grow.

Photography by Carl Murray
Illustration and Graphics by Stephanie Benson
Cover Design by Judy Petry
Edited by Liz McGehee

Even More ©
© Trudie Hughes, 1989

Printed in the United States of America
96 95 94 93 92 91 90 5 4 3 2 1

Library of Congress Cataloging-in-Publication Data

Hughes, Trudie
    Even more.

    1. Machine quilting--Patterns. 2. Patch-
work--Patterns. I. Title.
TT835.H83 1989   746.46   88-51093
ISBN 0-943574-53-6

Contents

Introduction

This book is an extension of the ideas presented in *Template-Free Quiltmaking* and *More Template-Free Quilt-making*. My main focus in this book is still on traditional quilt designs, but I do like to include those with a new twist. Many old quilts have common ingredients, which are easy to identify. The more you work with the same basic parts, and the more comfortable you become with cutting and sewing techniques, the easier it gets to experiment with variations of these designs.

The quilts in this book fall basically into two categories:

1. Quilts that are made from blocks.

2. Quilts whose design appears only after rows are joined. These are especially fun to make because the design "grows" as you piece.

The quilt designs are written "recipe style" and in various sizes. I have tried to simplify cutting and piecing instructions so that these quilts will be easier to make. My best advice to you is to read carefully, cut and sew accurately, and most of all, have fun.

Tools and Rules

Equipment

The secret to template-free quiltmaking is the equipment you use. With the right equipment and techniques, this type of quiltmaking can be accurate as well as fast.

The first thing you will need is a rotary cutter. It comes in two sizes, but I recommend the larger heavy-duty one. It is much easier to use and gives you better control. When the cutters first came out, they did not have a good cutting surface, and I almost gave up on them. Then Olfa™ came out with its mat, and it made all the difference in the world. The matte finish helps hold the fabric in place, making it easy to cut on. Also, the mat protects the blade and the table you are cutting on. A mat that allows you to cut the fabric as it comes off the bolt is the best size (approximately 18″ x 24″).

You will also need a tool, both to measure and to guide your cutter, ensuring a clean, straight cut. The Rotary Rule™ is a cutting tool designed for use in template-free quiltmaking. It has a ruler down its length and is graduated in ¼″ increments across its width so that you can measure right to left. To do more advanced procedures, it is very handy to have 45-degree angle markings and even nicer to have 60-degree angles printed on it. The Rotary Rule™ has three perpendicular intersecting lines across its width to help you subcut strips with straight square cuts. Dotted lines appear on some of the ⅛″ lines. These lines make short work of cutting accurate triangles.

In addition to the Rotary Rule™, I have developed a smaller ruler, the Rotary Mate™, which has many functions. First of all, it extends the 3½″ of the Rotary Rule™ to 7″ for wider cuts. It also has markings for additional fast triangles, but best of all, it has "Speedies" along one edge to make Snowball blocks and similar shapes with ease. My students have found that the 12″ length is easy to handle, and that once the fabric has been straightened, strips are easier to cut with the smaller ruler.

In addition to these tools, I find a right triangle very helpful. One that is 12″ on a side is the most useful. I like my fluorescent colored one, because when my sewing room looks like a rummage sale, it is easy to find.

It is so important to work with the best tools possible. "The right tool for the right job" is true. Shortcutting some of the tedious procedures in quilting gets you to the more enjoyable parts faster.

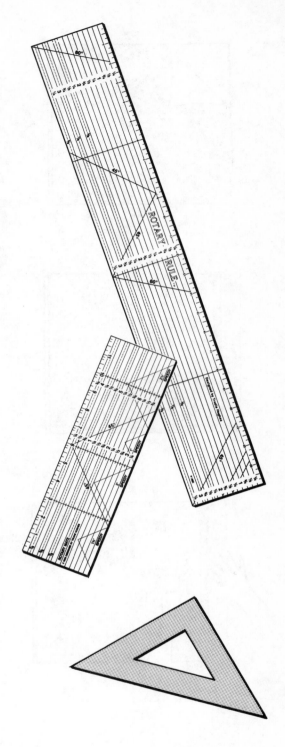

The ROTARY RULE™ and ROTARY MATE™ are available through Patched Works, 890 Elm Grove Rd., Elm Grove, Wisconsin 53122.

Slice and Dice

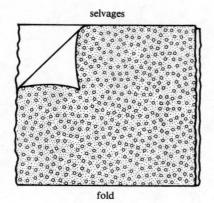

selvages

fold

It is important to learn to use a rotary cutter accurately and efficiently. Since you want to work with straight pieces, you must learn to cut perfectly straight strips.

The first step is to straighten the fabric. Threads in fabric are often far from perpendicular these days, making it almost impossible to truly straighten fabric. So we will be working with "close grain." You will need to make clean cuts, rather than cuts that are exactly on the straight of grain.

1. Fold fabric in half, selvage to selvage, the way it comes off the bolt.

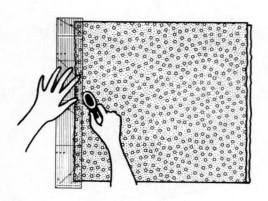

selvages

fold

2. Lay triangle along folded edge of fabric and push against right side of ruler until you are just at edge. (If you are right-handed, the bulk of the fabric should be coming from the right.)

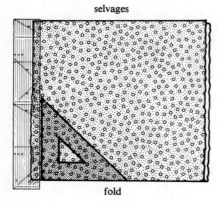

3. Hold ruler down with your left hand and begin cutting slightly in front of fold. Walk your hand up parallel with cutter and continue to cut off end of fabric. If you try to hold onto ruler at the bottom and cut to the end of it, you most likely will move it and therefore cut inaccurately. This is the only time you will have to cut such a long slice.

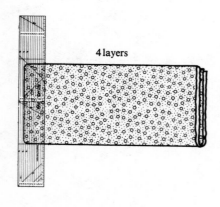

4 layers

4. Then, fold the fabric one more time, lining up cut edges. Using markings on ruler, cut appropriate strip width. Now cuts can be made only 11″ long, which is much easier. Check about every 18″ along length of fabric to see if you are still straight. Open up fabric and use triangle and ruler again to make sure you are still perpendicular to first fold.

If cuts are not perpendicular to fold, strips will have V shapes when you open them up. Everything is cut selvage to selvage, so you soon will become aware of this.

When you need to cut fabric wider than 3½″, you can combine width of ruler with any portion of the Rotary Mate™. You will find most cuts in this book are 3½″ or less. If you have cuts wider than the two rulers combined, use side of longer ruler to measure off desired width.

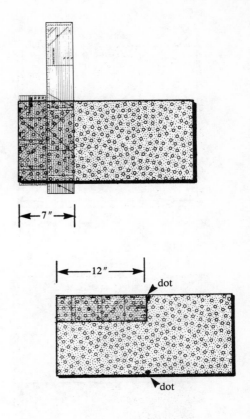

Subcutting into Squares and Rectangles

Some designs will require independent squares or rectangles. These "loose" units will be cut from strips.

Cut strips the width of unit plus seam allowances. Then, working with at least four layers at a time, straighten left edge of strips (usually has selvages and maybe a fold) by placing cut edge on halfway line of ruler and making a perpendicular slice.

Then, measure left to right, cutting squares same width as strips.

Rectangles are measured by using long side of ruler.

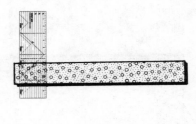

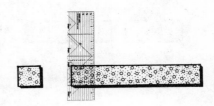

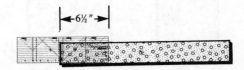

How to Cut Triangles

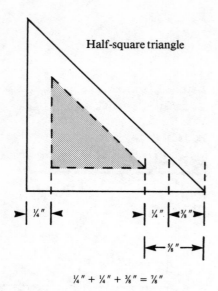

Half-square triangle

¼″   ¼″ ⅜″

⅝″

¼″ + ¼″ + ⅜″ = ⅞″

HALF-SQUARE TRIANGLES

A half-square triangle is half of a square and is measured on the two shorter sides. These sides are on grain.

If you were to draft a triangle on a piece of graph paper and add a ¼″ seam allowance all around, you would find an interesting phenomenon. The difference between the finished edges of the triangle and the cut edges with the seam allowance is not what you would expect. The straight side has ¼″ difference, yet the pointed side has ⅜″ difference between the finished and the cut point. You would expect ¼″, yet there is an additional ⅜″. Therefore, when making triangles, remember: The formula for half-square triangles is the finished size plus ⅞″.

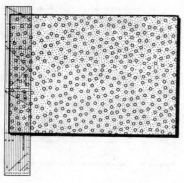

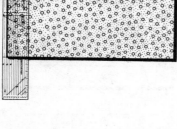

Cut a strip the desired finished measurement plus ⅞″.

4 layers

Then subcut into squares with the same measurement.

Take a stack of four squares and cut diagonally corner to corner once. These triangles are now the right size to mix with the other shapes.

QUARTER-SQUARE TRIANGLES

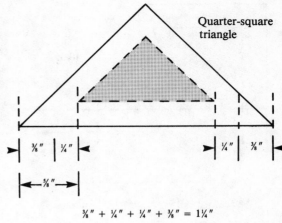

Quarter-square triangle

When a square is subdivided into four triangles, these triangles are referred to as quarter-square triangles. A quarter-square triangle is a right triangle that has the long side on grain. It is with this measurement that you will be concerned. You need to make this distinction in the use of these triangles because the outside edge of every square and the outside edge of every quilt is easier to handle if on grain.

If you draw a quarter-square triangle on graph paper, putting the long side on grain and drawing the seam allowance, you will find two points with ⅜″ sticking out from the finished points. The sum of these is 1¼″. So, the formula for dealing with a quarter-square triangle is the finished measurement of the long side plus 1¼″.

$$⅜″ + ¼″ + ¼″ + ⅜″ = 1¼″$$

If quarter-square triangles are cut and used independently: Cut a strip the desired finished measurement plus 1¼″.

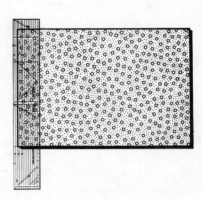

Then subcut into squares with the same measurement.

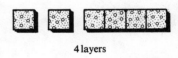

4 layers

With a stack of these squares (at least four), cut an X by lining up the ruler from corner to opposite corner. Without moving these pieces, cut in the other direction. Each square will yield four triangles with the long side on grain.

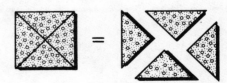

How to Cut Trapezoids

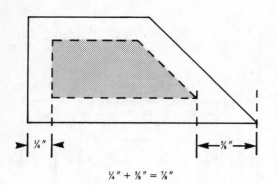

¼″ + ⅝″ = ⅞″

In making quilts with the kind of trapezoid shown here, I discovered that the same math used for half-square triangles also could be used for these trapezoids. Simply add ⅞″ to the length of the long side. Cut strips the width of trapezoid plus seam allowances.

Measure and mark the finished side plus ⅞″.

Working with four layers (right sides of fabric facing up), cut left edge perpendicular with top and bottom edges. From left edge, measure finished edge of long side plus ⅞″.

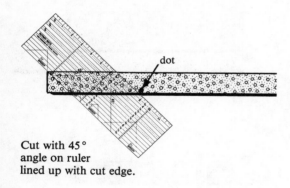

Cut with 45° angle on ruler lined up with cut edge.

Cut again with 45-degree mark on ruler. It does make a difference where you begin; the point of the trapezoid will go in one direction if you begin at top cut edge, and in opposite direction if you begin at bottom cut edge.

The next cut does not have to be marked. Measure the desired amount and make a straight cut.

How to Cut
"Decapitated Triangles"

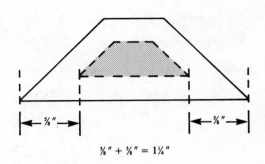

Although this shape is really a trapezoid, I refer to it as a "decapitated triangle" to help you form a mental picture of the shape you will need to cut. These shapes remind me of a quarter-square triangle with its tip cut off. The math is the same: measure the long side and add 1¼".

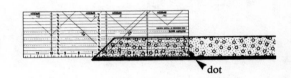

Using the Rotary Rule™, align the 45-degree angle marking with top edge of strip. Cut.

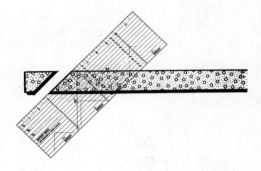

Measure along edge of strip until you get to desired long side, plus 1¼" seam allowance. Mark.

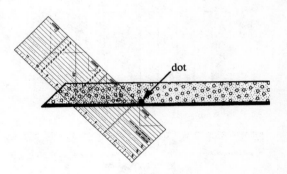

Line up ruler with dot and cut a 45-degree angle in opposite direction.

Point is then established for next cut.

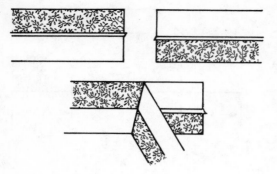

Subcutting Sewn Strips

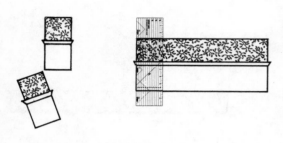

Many designs begin merely as cut strips. These strips are sewn together, pressed, and then cut again. Four patches and nine patches are best pieced this way, and these units occur over and over in other pieced blocks.

In a four patch, sew together two sets of contrasting strips.

Press consistently toward the same color.

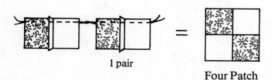

Then, place these two sets of sewn strips right sides together. Because of your pressing, you will find seam allowances already going in opposite directions.

Trim the selvages off and cut in pairs from left to right. When you sew these pairs together, there is no need to match or layer; they are ready to feed through the sewing machine in chain fashion.

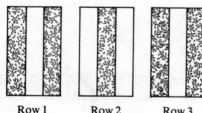

1 pair   Four Patch

In a nine patch, the same technique is used. However, now you have three sets of three sewn strips.

Place rows 1 and 2 together. Cut into pairs and sew together in chain fashion.

Cut Row 3 by itself.

Then, sew these three rows together.

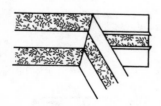

Row 1   Row 2   Row 3

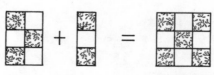

Nine patch

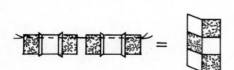

Hints

Whenever I thought it appropriate, I have included a symbol in the pattern that looks like the one on the right. It may be to warn you of a difficult intersection to piece, or just to remind you of how to cut a particular shape.

It is important to sew accurately after your pieces are cut. No one enjoys resewing to make things come out correctly. When I see work that looks sloppy or haphazardly pieced, I know it was inaccurately cut or improperly sewn. The techniques in my book use precision cutting and precision piecing. There is no trimming when things don't match, no stretching when things don't fit, and no recutting to adjust for piecing.

Here are three guidelines that I feel are most important:

1. Sew the proper seam allowance. Have you pieced something, only to have it turn out too small? Have you had to stretch pieces to get them to fit? To successfully complete the patterns in this book, you must be able to sew the proper seam allowance. The directions tell you what each step of the quilt will measure. If your seams differ, you will have to re-measure your own borders, etc. To make sure your seam allowances are correct, you may want to give yourself a sewing test.

SEWING TEST

About two years ago, I decided to do a study of students and their seam allowances. As a result, I have devised a test that you can take to determine where you must keep your eye when sewing. Many people assume that the edge of their presser foot is ¼″ from their needle. This is rarely true. Not only that, the proper seam allowance is not really ¼″. It is a **scant** ¼″.

Take three pieces of fabric 1½″ wide by about 5″ long. Sew these three pieces side by side with what you believe to be the correct seam allowance. Measure from edge to edge across the width of the piece. It should measure 3½″. Most students tend to take too large of a seam and they lose anywhere from ⅛″ to ¼″ in this piece that has only two seams. What happens in blocks where you have up to seven seams?

You must adjust your sewing so that the right measurement results. For some, this will mean having your fabric up under the presser foot. For others, it will mean lining up the fabric with the feed dog, and some of you will be lucky enough to have a machine that lets you adjust your needle position.

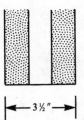

3½″

The patterns in this book assume that you will sew correctly. The more pieces in a quilt, and the smaller the pieces, the more important the precision.

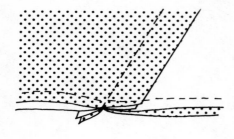

2. When coming to intersecting seams, seam allowances should always lie in opposite directions. Your machine wants to jog any bulky areas. If you line up all seams on the same side, it will most likely move one. By having seams in opposite directions, the bulk is reduced and seams hug the intersection. You want this intersection to look crisp from the front. It is not unusual in machine piecing to have seams twist and change directions, in order to make seam allowances go in opposite directions.

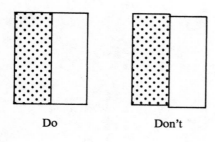

Do   Don't

3. When sewing two pieces together that should match, make sure they begin and end matched. All machines have a tendency to shift layers of fabric. If you think of your machine as an opponent that is purposely trying to shift everything, then you will hold on and make sure it doesn't. I do not pin, but if you feel it will ensure that the pieces match, by all means, pin.

Yardage

In planning the yardage for these quilts, I figured all fabric to have 42 usable inches. Once the yardage was calculated, I rounded it up to the nearest fraction of a yard.

Since I own a quilt shop, I have seen what happens when your yardage is figured too closely. Most quilters would rather have a little bit left over to add to a scrap quilt or as a fudge factor in case something is cut incorrectly. Several quilts in my books make use of these leftovers.

In the yardage requirements, fabric is broken down as to function. That way, you can substitute different fabrics for the border, binding, etc. You may not want to add the pieced borders, so that yardage can easily be eliminated.

I have found that the most efficient way to cut shapes from strips is to fold strips only once. Several strips can be layered and cut.

In figuring the yardage for the backs of these quilts, I tried to plan the most efficient use of your fabric. Therefore, sometimes it is pieced cross-grain, and sometimes it is pieced lengthwise.

Borders

All borders in the patterns are planned to be cut cross-grain. Therefore, the number of strips needed for a plain border are specified in the cutting instructions. If you want to cut your borders lengthwise, disregard these instructions and add to the yardage required.

If a border is to be pieced, don't piece the strips with the short ends together. Instead, lay them in an **L** shape and sew from where they intersect, to where they intersect. This slanted seam is more difficult to spot. To piece borders, sew all strips together and measure off this long strip. This will result in seams falling in different places on the quilt, making them harder to spot as well. The only time I worry about where the seams fall is when they get too close to the corners.

I have designed the borders to be cut to length and sewn on blunted. I find, especially in handling pieced borders, that the quilt stays more ''squared'' with this type border. If you are not careful with mitered borders, the outside dimensions may differ. However, if you do prefer to miter your borders, you will have to cut more strips and add on to the planned yardage. The best way to sew on these borders is to establish the center of both the border and the quilt, then match ends and centers.

Several of the quilts in this book have pieced borders. These are not necessary if you do not want to tackle them; just make plain borders instead.

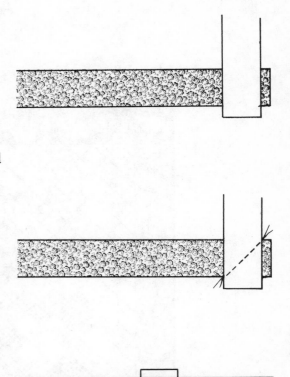

Evening Star
with plain border.

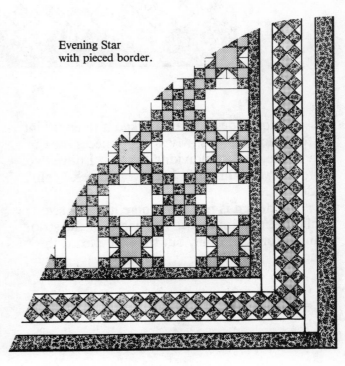

Evening Star
with pieced border.

ALBUM QUILT

This quilt design has sparked a renewed interest for many quilters. My version pieces the quilt as a whole, not as individual blocks. I have had more fun with this quilt lately; one week I think I made six.

The design is presented here in three sizes: miniature, crib, and lap. The width of the strip changes for each quilt, but they are pieced the same.

Miniature Quilt

Pieced area finishes to 16″ square.
After border, quilt will be 20″ square.

Fabric A
Fabric B
Fabric C
Fabric D

FABRIC REQUIREMENTS

Background (A)—½ yd.
9 assorted fabrics for blocks (B)—1 strip each 1¼″
    wide by 42″ long
Pieced border (C)—¼ yd.
Outer border (D)—⅜ yd.
Binding—⅓ yd.
Backing—¾ yd.

CUTTING INSTRUCTIONS

Background (A)

1. Cut 3 strips 1¼″ wide. From these, cut 60 squares 1¼″, and cut 11 rectangles 2¾″ by 1¼″.
2. Cut 3 strips 1¼″ wide for pieced border.
3. Cut 3 strips 2″ wide for pieced border.

Assorted fabrics (B)

1. Cut 1 strip 1¼″ wide of each fabric.
2. Cut 2 squares 1¼″, 6 rectangles 1¼″ by 2″, and 2 rectangles 1¼″ by 2¾″.

Pieced border (C)

Cut 3 strips 1¼″ wide.

Outer border (D)

Cut 4 strips 2½″ wide.

Binding

Cut 4 strips 2″ wide.

PIECING AND ASSEMBLY

1. Sew 3 sets of strips that look like this:

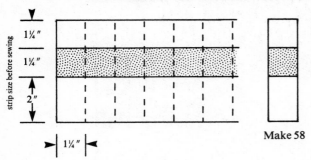

Make 58

Press seams toward darker fabric. Make cuts every 1¼″. You will need 58 of these little pieced units. These strips will begin and end each row.

2. Piece 2 corner units that look like this:

You can take these pieces from border set-ups or you can cut them just for corner units.

3. Starting in a corner, piece in diagonal rows. Be careful with seam allowance so strips will be the right length when pieced. If you keep all seams toward darker fabrics, seam allowances will be going opposite directions at intersections. Press after each row is added.

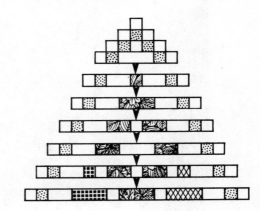

4. After quilt top is pieced, draw a line ¼″ away from points of squares. **Do not cut off these points until border is sewn on!**

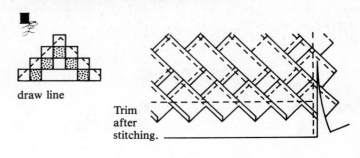

draw line

Trim after stitching.

5. Take the 2½″ wide border strips (D) and measure off 2 strips 16½″ long. Sew to top and bottom. Press. Measure off 2 strips 20½″ long and sew to sides. Press.

Crib Quilt

Pieced area finishes to 31¾″ by 40¼″.
After last border, quilt will be 37¾″ by 46¼″.

Fabric A
Fabric B
Fabric C
Fabric D

FABRIC REQUIREMENTS

Background (A)—1¼ yd.
12 assorted fabrics (B)—1 strip each 2″ wide and
    42″ long
Pieced border (C)—⅜ yd.
Outer border (D)—⅝ yd.
Binding—½ yd.
Backing—1½ yds.

CUTTING INSTRUCTIONS

Background (A)

1. Cut 6 strips 2″ wide. Cut into 83 squares
2″ and 14 rectangles 2″ by 5″.
2. Cut 4 strips 2″ wide for pieced border.
3. Cut 4 strips 3½″ wide for pieced borders.

Assorted fabrics (B)

Cut 1 strip 2″ wide of each fabric. From this
strip, cut 2 squares 2″, 6 rectangles 2″ by 3½″,
and 2 rectangles 2″ by 5″.

Pieced border (C)

Cut 4 strips 2″ wide.

Outer border (D)

Cut 5 strips 3½″ wide.

Binding

Cut 5 strips 2½″ wide.

PIECING AND ASSEMBLY

1. For pieced border, make 4 sets of strips
that look like this:

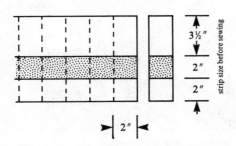

Make cuts every 2″. You will need 64 units. These
will begin and end each row.

2. Piece 2 corner units that look like this:

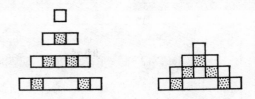

You can take these pieces from your border set-
ups or you can cut them just for corner units.

3. Starting in a corner, piece in diagonal
rows. Be careful with seam allowance so strips will
be the right length when pieced. If you keep all
seams toward darker fabrics, seam allowances will
be going opposite directions at intersections. Press
after each row is added.

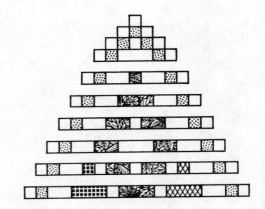

4. After quilt top is pieced, draw a line ¼″
away from points of squares. **Do not cut off these
points until border is sewn on!**

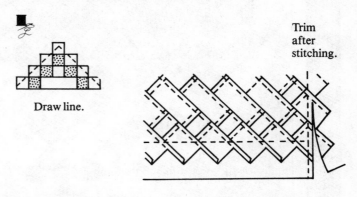

Draw line.

Trim
after
stitching.

5. Take the 3½″ wide strips of outer border
fabric (D) and measure off 2 strips 32¼″ long. Sew
to top and bottom. Piece remaining 3½″ wide
strips and measure off 2 strips 46¾″ long. Sew to
long sides. Press.

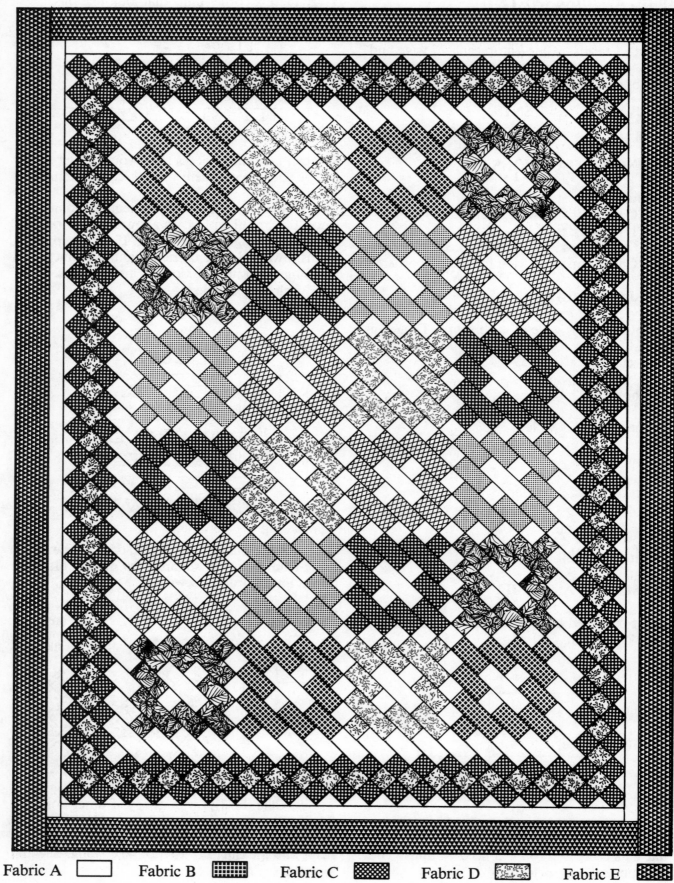

Fabric A   Fabric B   Fabric C   Fabric D   Fabric E

Lap Quilt

Pieced area finishes to 44½" by 61½".
After first border, quilt will be 47½" by 64½".
After second border, quilt will be 53½" by 70½".

FABRIC REQUIREMENTS

Background (A)—2 yds. (for piecing and first
    border)
24 assorted fabrics (B)—1 strip each at 2" wide
    and 42" long
Dark pieced border (C)—¾ yd.
Medium pieced border (D)—½ yd.
Outer border (E)—¾ yd.
Binding—⅝ yd.
Backing—3½ yd. (pieced crosswise)

CUTTING INSTRUCTIONS

Background (A)

1. Cut 13 strips 2" wide. From these strips,
cut 179 squares 2" and 26 rectangles 2" by 5".
2. Cut 5 strips 2" wide for pieced border.
3. Cut 5 strips 3½" wide for pieced border.
4. Cut 6 strips 2" wide for first border.

Assorted fabrics (B)

Cut 1 strip 2" wide from each fabric. Cut 2
squares 2", 6 rectangles 2" by 3½", and 2 rectangles 2" by 5".

Dark pieced border (C)

Cut 10 strips 2" wide.

Medium pieced border (D)

Cut 5 strips 2" wide.

Outer border (E)

Cut 7 strips 3½" wide.

Binding

Cut 7 strips 2½" wide.

PIECING AND ASSEMBLY

1. Piece 5 sets of strips that look like this:

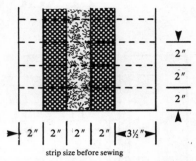

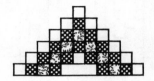

strip size before sewing

Make cuts every 2". You will need 96 units. These
will begin and end each row.

2. Piece 2 corner units that look like this:

You can take these pieces from your border set-
ups or you can cut them just for corner units.

3. Starting in a corner, piece in diagonal
rows. See illustration in Step 3 on page 19. Be
careful with your seam allowance so strips will be
right length when pieced. If you keep all seams
toward darker fabrics, seam allowances will be
going opposite directions at intersections. Press
after each row is added.

4. After quilt top is pieced, draw a line ¼"
away from points of squares. **Do not cut off these
points until border is sewn on!**

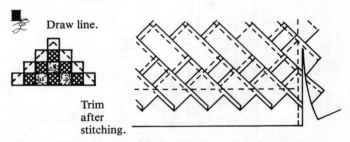

Draw line.

Trim
after
stitching.

5. Take 2" wide strips of background fabric
(A) and piece them together (on the slant) and
measure off 2 strips 45" long. Sew to short sides.
Press.
    Measure off 2 strips 65" long and sew to long
sides. Press.
6. Take 3½" wide strips of outer border fabric
(E) and piece together (on the slant). Measure off
2 strips 48" long and sew to top and bottom.
Press.
    Measure off 2 strips 71" long and sew to long
sides. Press.

BURGOYNE SURROUNDED

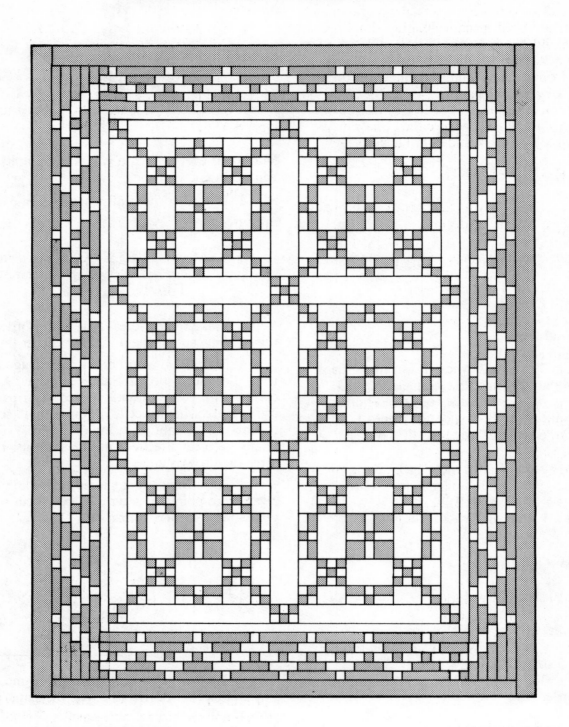

Lap Quilt

Fabric A ☐
Fabric B ▨

Pieced area finishes to 37″ by 55″.
After first border, quilt will be 39″ by 57″.
After pieced border, quilt will be 49″ by 67″.
After last border, quilt will be 53″ by 71″.

This simple, but stunning, quilt design has been around for centuries. I was always fascinated with it, yet not until speed techniques simplified the piecing did the quilt seem worth making. What finally convinced me to make it was the photograph of Donna Eines' quilt in Nancy Martin's *Pieces of the Past*. The added pieced border made the design too hard to resist. Most often you see this design with a light background. I have made samples with both dark and light backgrounds.

FABRIC REQUIREMENTS

Background (A)—3½ yds. (2½ yds. for piecing,
   1 yd. for pieced border)
Accent (B)—3½ yds. (1¼ yd. for piecing, 1 yd.
   for borders, 1¼ yd. for pieced border)
Binding—⅝ yd.
Backing—3½ yds. (pieced crosswise)

CUTTING INSTRUCTIONS

Background (A)

1. Cut 8 strips 1½" wide for nine patches.
2. Cut 2 strips 1½" wide for four patches.
3. Cut 4 strips 2½" wide for T units.
4. Cut 2 strips 1½" wide for T units and center blocks.
5. Cut 10 strips 3½" wide. From these cut 24 rectangles 5½" by 3½", 48 rectangles 2½" by 3½", and 7 rectangles 15½" by 3½".
6. Cut 5 strips 2½" wide. Cut into 10 rectangles 15½" by 2½".

For pieced border:

1. Cut 3 strips 3½" wide.
2. Cut 4 strips 2½" wide.
3. Cut 3 strips 1½" wide.
4. Cut 1 strip 1½" wide. Cut into 4 lengths 2½" wide and 2 squares 1½".

Accent (B)

1. Cut 10 strips 1½" wide for nine patches.
2. Cut 2 strips 1½" wide for four patches.
3. Cut 4 strips 2½" wide for T units and center blocks.
4. Cut 2 strips 1½" wide for T units and corner blocks.
5. Cut 5 strips 1½" wide for first border.
6. Cut 7 strips 2½" wide for last border.

For pieced border:

1. Cut 3 strips 5½" wide.
2. Cut 3 strips 3½" wide.
3. Cut 4 strips 1½" wide.
4. Cut 4 strips 1½" wide. Cut into 4 lengths 6½" long, 4 lengths 5½" long, 8 lengths 4½" long, 4 lengths 3½" long, 4 lengths 2½" long, and 4 squares 1½".

Binding

Cut 7 strips 2½" wide.

PIECING AND ASSEMBLY

1. TO MAKE NINE PATCHES: Using 1½" wide strips, make 2 of each of row 1 and row 2.

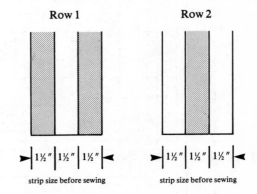

Row 1   Row 2

|← 1½" | 1½" | 1½" →|
strip size before sewing

Make 1 set of row 3.

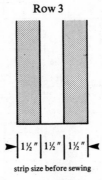

Row 3

|← 1½" | 1½" | 1½" →|
strip size before sewing

Cut every 1½". Sew rows 1 and 2 together. Set aside 6 units of partial nine patches for border. Then add row 3 to make 26 nine patches. (See page 12 for more information on cutting nine patches.)

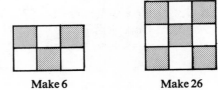

Make 6   Make 26

2. TO MAKE FOUR PATCHES: Make 2 sets of strips that look like this:

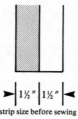

Place the 2 strips right sides together and cut every 1½". Sew into pairs. You will need 28 four patches.

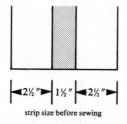

Make 28

3. TO MAKE T UNITS: Make 1 set of strips that looks like this:

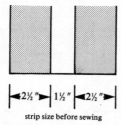

Make 1 set of strips that looks like this:

Place these strips right sides together. Cut every 1½". Sew into pairs. You will need 24 of these T units.

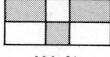

Make 24

4. TO MAKE BLOCK CENTERS: Make 1 set of strips that looks like this:

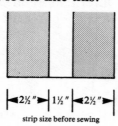

Make 12 cuts at 2½". Make 1 set of strips that looks like this:

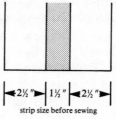

Make 6 cuts at 1½". Join in 3 rows to make 6 block centers that look like this:

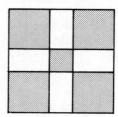

5. Assemble 5 rows to make 6 main blocks that look like this:

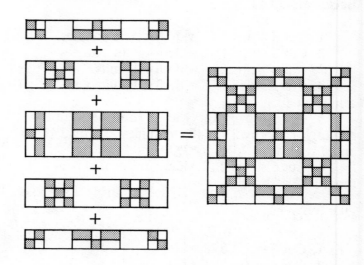

6. Sew 2 blocks across and 3 blocks down with 3½" by 15½" background strips. Between rows, alternate these lattice strips with nine patches.

7. Add border of 2½" by 15½" strips and partial nine patches according to illustration.

8. With 1½" wide strips of accent fabric (B), measure off 2 lengths of 37½" and sew to top and bottom. Press.

Piece remaining strips (on the slant) and measure off 2 lengths of 57½" and sew to long sides. Press.

CREATIVE OPTION

After adding first border, you may add a pieced border. This pieced border is made from 5 rows of strips.

1. For rows 1 and 5, make 3 sets of strips that look like this:

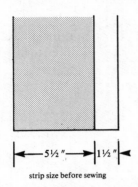

|←——— 5½" ———|←—1½"—|←

strip size before sewing

2. For rows 2 and 4, make 3 sets of strips that look like this:

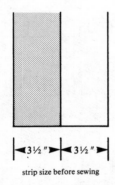

|←—3½"—|←—3½"—|

strip size before sewing

3. For row 3, make 1½ sets of strips that look like this:

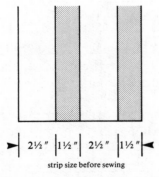

|← 2½" |1½"| 2½" |1½"|←

strip size before sewing

Each set of strips is 6½" wide. From each of these sets of strips, cut every 1½".

4. Sew these segments into rows, then sew the 5 rows together.

5. Make borders for top and bottom that look like this:

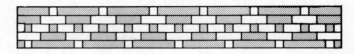

Pay special attention to beginning and ending of each row. There will be extra pieces on ends of each row. When sewn together, these rows will be 39½" long.

Sew to top and bottom. Press.

6. Make a border for each side that looks like this, referring to large diagram on page 22 for complete segment:

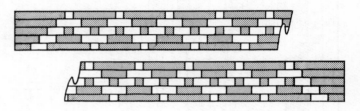

Pay special attention to beginning and ending of each row. When sewn together, these rows will be 67½" long. Sew to long sides. Press.

7. Piece 2½" wide strips of accent fabric (B) (on the slant) for last border. Measure off 2 lengths of 49½" and sew to top and bottom. Press.

Measure off 2 lengths of 71½" and sew to long sides. Press.

Fabric A
Fabric B

Large Quilt

Pieced area finishes to 73″ by 91″.
After first border, quilt will be 75″ by 93″.
After pieced border, quilt will be 85″ by 103″.
After last border, quilt will be 89″ by 107″.

FABRIC REQUIREMENTS

Background (A)—8 yds. (6¼ yds. for piecing,
  1 yd. for pieced border, ¾ yd. for first
  border)
Accent fabric (B)—4 ¾ yds. (2¼ yds for piecing,
  1 yd. for border, 1½ yds. for pieced border)
Binding—1 yd.
Backing—9½ yds.

CUTTING INSTRUCTIONS

Background (A)

1. Cut 16 strips 1½″ wide for nine patches.
2. Cut 6 strips 1½″ wide for four patches.
3. Cut 6 strips 2½″ wide for T units.
4. Cut 3 strips 1½″ wide for T units.
5. Cut 2 strips 2½″ wide for block centers.
6. Cut 3 strips 1½″ wide for block centers.
7. Cut 10 strips 3½″ wide. Cut these into 160 segments of 2½″ each.
8. Cut 7 strips 5½″ wide. Cut these into 80 segments of 3½″ each.
9. Cut 16 strips 3½″ wide. Cut these into 31 lengths 15½″ long.
10. Cut 9 strips 2½″ wide. Cut these into 18 lengths 15½″ long.
11. Cut 10 strips 1½″ wide for first border.

For pieced border:

1. Cut 4 strips 1½″ wide.
2. Cut 4 strips 3½″ wide.
3. Cut 4 strips 2½″ wide.
4. Cut 1 strip 1½″ wide. Cut into 4 lengths 2½″ long, and 4 squares 1½″.

Accent (B)

1. Cut 20 strips 1½″ wide for nine patches.
2. Cut 6 strips 1½″ wide for four patches.
3. Cut 6 strips 2½″ wide for T units.
4. Cut 3 strips 1½″ wide for T units.
5. Cut 6 strips 2½″ wide for block centers.
6. Cut 1 strip 1½″ wide for block centers.
7. Cut 12 strips 2½″ wide for last border.

For pieced border:

1. Cut 4 strips 5½″ wide.
2. Cut 4 strips 3½″ wide.
3. Cut 4 strips 1½″ wide.
4. Cut 4 strips 1½″ wide. Cut into 4 lengths 6½″ long, 4 lengths 5½″ long, 8 lengths 4½″ long, 4 lengths 3½″ long, 4 lengths 2½″ long, and 4 squares 1½″.

Binding

Cut 12 strips 2½″ wide.

PIECING AND ASSEMBLY

The easiest way to do this quilt is to make all ingredients first and then piece blocks, add sashing, and sew on borders.

1. TO MAKE NINE PATCHES: Using 1½″ wide strips, make 4 of each of the following sets of strips:

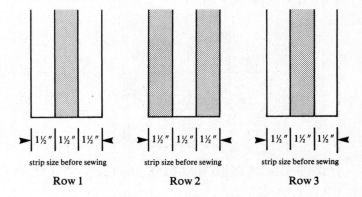

Row 1   Row 2   Row 3

Cut every 1½ ″. Sew rows 1 and 2 together. Set aside 14 units of partial nine patches for border.

Make 14

Then add row 3 to make 92 nine patches. (See page 12 for more information on making nine patches.)

Make 92

2. TO MAKE FOUR PATCHES: Using 1½″ wide strips, make 6 sets of strips that look like this:

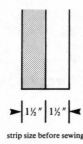

strip size before sewing

Place 2 sets of strips right sides together and cut every 1½ ″. Sew these pairs. You will need 84 Four Patches.

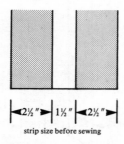

Make 84

3. TO MAKE T UNITS: Make 3 sets of strips that look like this:

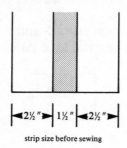

|◄2½ ″►| 1½ ″ |◄2½ ″►|

strip size before sewing

Make 3 sets of strips that look like this:

|◄2½ ″►| 1½ ″ |◄2½ ″►|

strip size before sewing

Place 1 set of each, right sides together, and cut every 1½ ″. Sew together, being careful to have seam allowances going in opposite directions at intersections. You will need 80 of these T units.

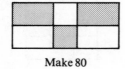

Make 80

4. TO MAKE BLOCK CENTERS: Make 3 sets of strips that look like this:

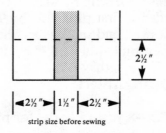

|◄2½ ″►| 1½ ″ |◄2½ ″►|

strip size before sewing

Cut every 2½ ″. Make 1 set of strips that looks like this:

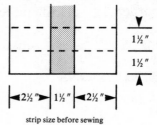

|◄2½ ″►| 1½ ″ |◄2½ ″►|

strip size before sewing

Cut every 1½ ″. Join in 3 rows to make 20 block centers that look like this:

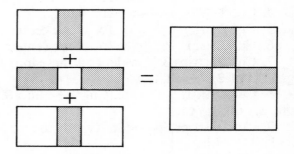

5. Assemble 5 rows to make 20 blocks that look like this:

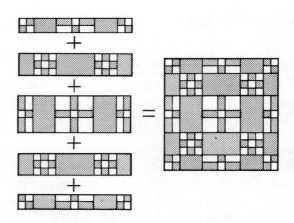

6. Sew 4 blocks across and 5 blocks down with 3½ ″ by 15½ ″ sashing between blocks in rows. Alternate sashing and nine patches to sew in between rows.

7. Add border of 2½" by 15½" strips and partial nine patches according to illustration.

8. Piece 1½" wide strips of background fabric (A) (on the slant) for first plain border. Measure off 2 lengths of 73½" and sew to top and bottom. Press.

Measure off 2 lengths of 93½" and sew to long sides. Press.

CREATIVE OPTION

After adding first border, you may add a pieced border. This pieced border is made from 5 rows of strips.

1. For rows 1 and 5, make 4 sets of strips that look like this:

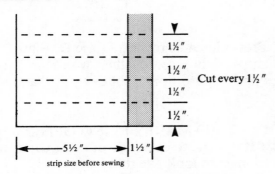

2. For rows 2 and 4, make 4 sets of strips that look like this:

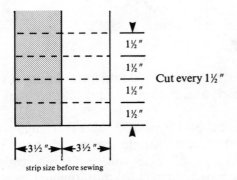

3. For row 3, make 2 sets of strips that look like this:

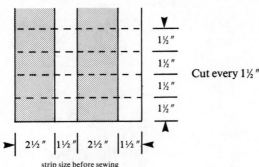

Each set of strips is 6½" wide.

4. Sew these segments into rows, then sew rows together.

5. Make 2 borders for top and bottom that look like this, referring to large diagram on page 26 for complete segment:

Pay special attention to beginning and ending of each row. There will be extra pieces on ends of each row. When sewn together, these rows will be 75½" long.

Sew to top and bottom. Press.

6. Make a border for each side that looks like this, referring to the large diagram on page 26 for the complete segment.

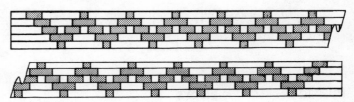

You will have to pay special attention to beginning and ending of each row. There will be extra pieces on ends of each row. When sewn together, these rows will be 103½" long. Sew to long sides. Press.

7. Piece 2½" wide strips of accent fabric (B) (on the slant) for last border. Measure off 2 lengths of 85½" and sew to top and bottom. Press. Measure off 2 lengths of 107½" and sew to long sides. Press.

JACOB'S ELEVATOR

This quilt pattern has no relation to the Jacob's Ladder quilt design. I just felt a more whimsical name was in order. This dramatic quilt is made up of such simple ingredients that it can be pieced very quickly. There are four basic units to assemble first. Then the quilt is put together in rows across the width of the quilt. It isn't until rows are joined that the quilt design emerges.

I found this quilt to be a good exercise in piecing tricky units. Flying Geese units and Square-in-a-Square units are frustrating if you are careless with your piecing. Tips are offered to help you master this problem.

The four basic units used in this quilt are:

Four Patches

Puss-in-the-Corner blocks

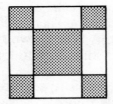

Flying Geese units

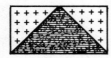

Square-in-a-Square blocks

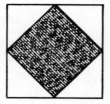

Piecing Instructions for Both Sizes

1. TO MAKE FOUR PATCHES: Make sets of strips that look like this:

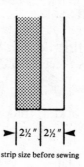

2½″ 2½″
strip size before sewing

Press all seams toward fabric D. Place 2 sets of strips, right sides together, with seams going in opposite directions. Cut every 2½″ and sew in pairs.

2. TO MAKE FLYING GEESE UNITS: Sew a B triangle to each side of a C quarter-square triangle to look like this:

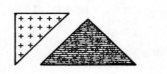
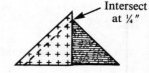

Intersect at ¼″

HINT: Sew 1 side on first, lining it up at pointed end, and making sure it intersects at ¼″.

Press and then add second triangle. When sewing on second triangle, be sure that top point intersects at ¼″. This will result in a straight edge at top with correct seam allowance remaining.

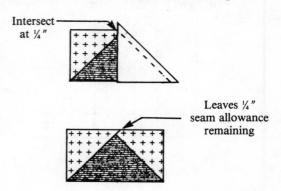

Intersect at ¼″

Leaves ¼″ seam allowance remaining

3. TO MAKE PUSS-IN-THE-CORNER BLOCKS: Make sets of strips that look like this:

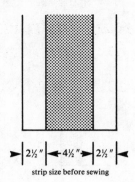

2½" 4½" 2½"
strip size before sewing

Press all seams toward fabric D. Cut every 2½". 4"

Make sets of strips that look like this:

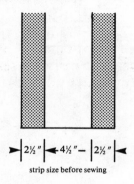

2½" 4½" − 2½"
strip size before sewing

Press all seams toward fabric D. Cut every 4½". 2"

Sew these units together to make blocks that look like this:

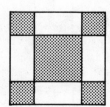

4. TO MAKE SQUARE-IN-A-SQUARE BLOCKS: Sew an A triangle onto all sides of center square.

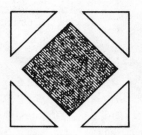

Intersect at ¼"

HINT: When sewing, place triangle as underneath layer, making sure points stick out ⅜" so that seams intersect at ¼". Press. Sew on remaining triangles, making sure beginning and ending edges intersect at ¼".

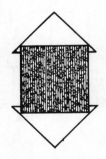
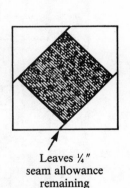
Leaves ¼" seam allowance remaining

This quilt is pieced in rows across quilt. You will be alternating wide rows with narrow rows. Follow illustrations to piece correct layout.

Lap Quilt

Pieced area finishes to 40″ by 64″.
After first border, quilt will be 43″ by 67″.
After second border, quilt will be 48″ by 72″.
After third border, quilt will be 55″ by 79″.

Fabric A
Fabric B
Fabric C
Fabric D

FABRIC REQUIREMENTS

Fabric A—1 yd.	First border—½ yd.
Fabric B—⅞ yd.	Second border—¾ yd.
Fabric C—1¼ yd.	Third border—1 yd.
Fabric D—⅝ yd.	Binding—¾ yd.
	Backing—4¾ yds.

CUTTING INSTRUCTIONS

Fabric A

1. Cut 3 strips 2½″ wide for Four Patches.
2. Cut 1 strip 4½″ wide for Puss-in-the-Corner blocks.
3. Cut 2 strips 2½″ wide for Puss-in-the-Corner blocks.
4. Cut 2 strips 4⅞″ wide. Cut these into 16 squares 4⅞″. Cut these diagonally to yield 32 triangles for Square-in-a-Square blocks.

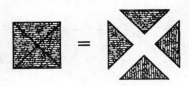

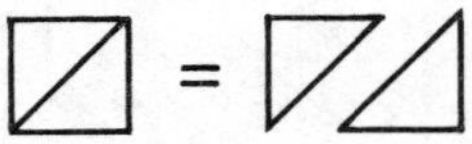

Fabric B

Cut 5 strips 4⅞″ wide. Cut into 38 squares 4⅞″. Cut these diagonally to yield 76 triangles for Flying Geese units.

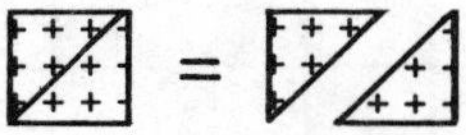

Fabric C

1. Cut 3 strips 9¼″ wide. Cut into 10 squares 9¼″. Cut these squares with an X to yield 38 quarter-square triangles for Flying Geese units.
2. Cut 2 strips 6⅛″ wide. Cut into 8 squares 6⅛″ for Square-in-a-Square blocks.

Fabric D

1. Cut 5 strips 2½″ wide for Four Patches and Puss-in-the-Corner blocks.
2. Cut 1 strip 4½″ wide for Puss-in-the-Corner blocks.

First border

Cut 6 strips 2″ wide.

Second border

Cut 7 strips 3″ wide.

Third border

Cut 8 strips 4″ wide.

Binding

Cut 8 strips 2½″ wide.

PIECING AND ASSEMBLY

1. Make 24 Four Patches that look like this:

These should measure 4½″ from raw edge to raw edge.

2. Make 38 Flying Geese units that look like this:

These should measure 4½″ by 8½″ from raw edge to raw edge.

3. Make 7 Puss-in-the-Corner blocks that look like this:

These should measure 8½″ from raw edge to raw edge.

4. Make 8 Square-in-a-Square blocks that look like this:

These should measure 8½″ from raw edge to raw edge.

5. Follow illustration to assemble quilt.
6. Take 2″ wide strips of first border fabric and measure off 2 strips 40½″ long and sew to top and bottom. Press.
Piece remaining 2″ wide strips (on the slant) and measure off 2 strips 67½″ long. Sew to long sides and press.
7. Piece 3″ wide strips of second border fabric (on the slant) and measure off 2 strips 43½″ long. Sew to top and bottom. Press.
Measure off 2 strips 72½″ long and sew to long sides. Press.
8. Piece 4″ wide strips of third border fabric (on the slant) and measure off 2 strips 48½″ long. Sew to top and bottom. Press.
Measure off 2 strips 79½″ long and sew to long sides. Press.

Fabric A 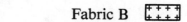   Fabric B   Fabric C   Fabric D

Large Quilt

Pieced area finishes to 64″ by 88″.
After first border, quilt will be 72″ by 96″.
After second border, quilt will be 76″ by 100″.
After third border, quilt will be 84″ by 108″.

FABRIC REQUIREMENTS

Fabric A—1¾ yds.	First and third border—3⅜ yds.
Fabric B—1¾ yds.	Second border—¾ yd.
Fabric C—2¼ yds.	Binding—1 yd.
Fabric D—1⅛ yds.	Backing—9½ yds.

CUTTING INSTRUCTIONS

Fabric A

1. Cut 6 strips 2½″ wide for Four Patches.
2. Cut 2 strips 4½″ wide for Puss-in-the-Corner blocks.
3. Cut 4 strips 2½″ wide for Puss-in-the-Corner blocks.
4. Cut 5 strips 4⅞″ wide. Cut into 36 squares 4⅞″. Cut these diagonally to yield 72 triangles for Square-in-a-Square blocks.

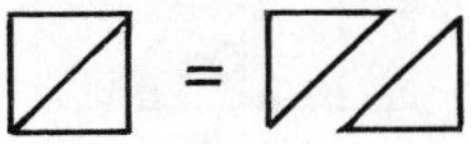

Fabric B

Cut 11 strips 4⅞″ wide. Cut into 82 squares 4⅞″. Cut these diagonally to yield 164 triangles for Flying Geese units.

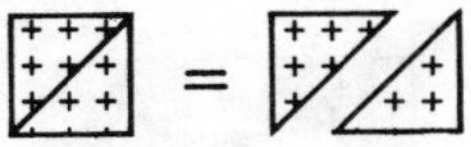

Fabric C

1. Cut 6 strips 9¼″ wide. Cut into 21 squares 9¼″. Cut these squares with an X to yield 82 quarter-square triangles for Flying Geese units.

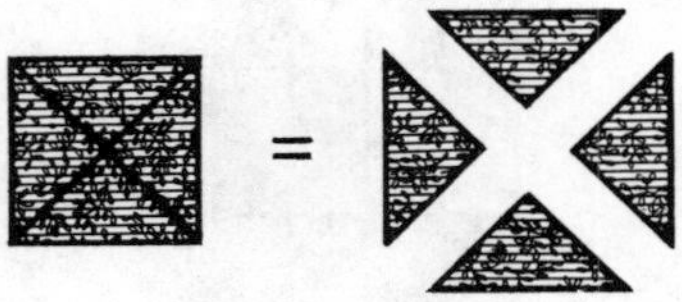

2. Cut 3 strips 6⅛″ wide. Cut these into 18 squares 6⅛″ for Square-in-a-Square blocks.

Fabric D

1. Cut 10 strips 2½″ wide for Puss-in-the-Corner blocks and Four Patches.
2. Cut 2 strips 4½″ wide for Puss-in-the-Corner blocks.

First and third borders

Cut 8 lengthwise strips 4½″ wide.

Second border

Cut 9 strips 2½″ wide.

Binding

Cut 11 strips 2½″ wide.

PIECING AND ASSEMBLY

1. Make 48 Four Patches that look like this:

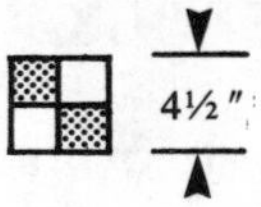

2. Make 82 Flying Geese units that look like this:

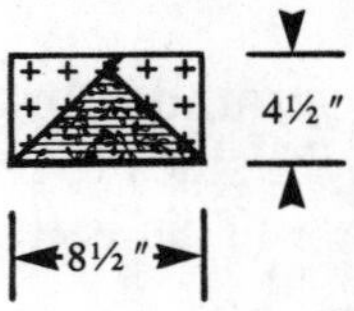

3. Make 17 Puss-in-the-Corner blocks that look like this:

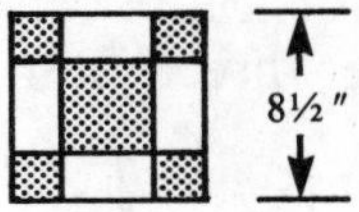

4. Make 18 Square-in-a-Square blocks that look like this:

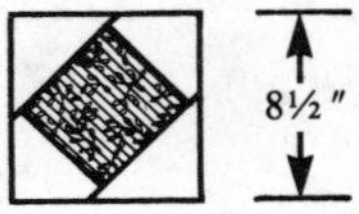

5. Follow illustration to assemble quilt.
6. With 4½″ wide strips for first border, measure off 2 strips of 64½″ and sew to top and bottom. Press.
   Measure off 2 strips, each 96½″ and sew to long sides. Press.
7. Piece 2½″ wide strips for second border (on the slant). Measure off 2 strips 72½″ long and sew to top and bottom. Press.
   Measure off 2 strips 100½″ long and sew to long sides. Press.
8. With 4½″ wide strips for third border, measure off 2 strips 76½″ long and sew to top and bottom. Press.
   Measure off 2 strips 108½″ long and sew to long sides. Press.

EVENING IN IRELAND

After reading *A Dozen Variables* by Marsha McCloskey and Nancy J. Martin, I began experimenting with other blocks that could be mixed with the Variable Star block. Here is a version, mixing the Variable Star with an Irish Chain. Instead of alternating two blocks, you will be using three different blocks.

Piecing Instructions for All Sizes

VARIABLE STAR BLOCK

This block is made from half-square triangle units and squares. I prefer to make the triangle units with "fast triangles."

1. Place background fabric (A) and double chain fabric (B) right sides together and mark a grid of squares 2⅜". (This is the first dotted line on the Rotary Rule™.)

2. Mark a diagonal line through these squares, first 1 direction in every other row of squares, then other direction in unmarked squares.

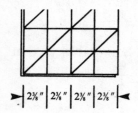

3. Stitch a ¼" seam on each side of this diagonal line. Cut apart and press. At this step, these squares should measure 2" from raw edge to raw edge.

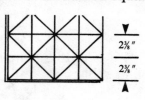

4. This star is pieced in 3 rows:

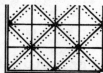

Row 1
Row 2
Row 3

When the star block is completed, it should measure 6½" square, from raw edge to raw edge.

PUSS-IN-THE-CORNER BLOCK

1. Make sets of strips that look like this:

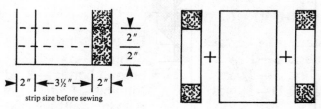

Cut every 2".

2. Sew 1 of these units onto each side of large rectangle.

These blocks should measure 8" by 6½" from raw edge to raw edge.

FIVE-PATCH BLOCK

1. Make 3 sets of strips that look like this:

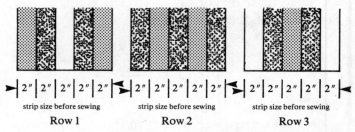

Row 1
Row 2
Row 3

2. Place row 1 and row 2 right sides together and cut every 2". Sew together in pairs. Each block will use 2 of these pairs.

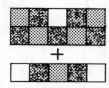

Take row 3 and cut every 2". Sew between 2 pairs of rows 1 and 2.

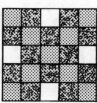

These blocks should measure 8" square from raw edge to raw edge.

Odd-numbered rows will alternate Variable Star blocks and Puss-in-the-Corner blocks. Even-numbered rows will alternate Puss-in-the-Corner blocks and Five-Patch blocks.

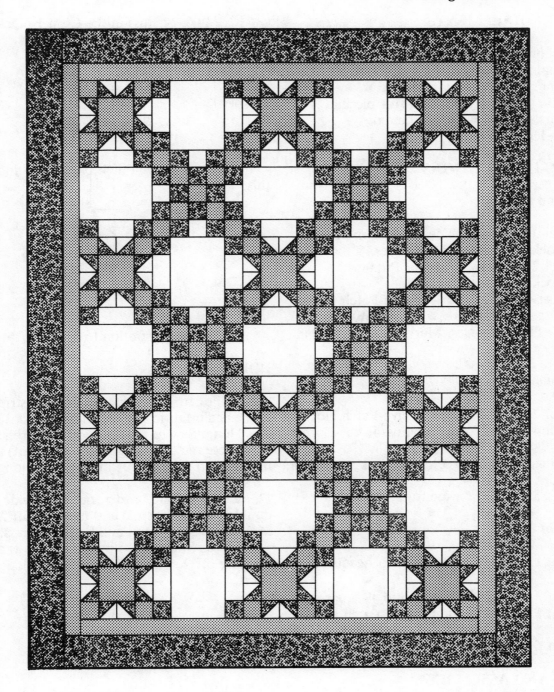

Crib Quilt

Pieced area finishes to 33″ by 46½″.
After first border, quilt will be 36″ by 49½″.
After last border, quilt will be 42″ by 55½″.

Fabric A
Fabric B
Fabric C

FABRIC REQUIREMENTS

Background (A)—1⅛ yds.
Double chain and star (B)—1⅞ yds. (1¼ yds. for
    piecing, ⅝ yd. for second border)
Single chain (C)—1¾ yds. (¾ yd. for piecing, ½ yd.
    for first border, ½ yd. for binding)
Backing—1¾ yds.

CUTTING INSTRUCTIONS

Background (A)

1. Cut 3 strips 6½" wide for Puss-in-the-
Corner blocks. Cut into 17 rectangles, 5" by 6½".
2. Cut 2 strips 3½" wide for Puss-in-the-
Corner blocks.
3. Cut 3 strips 2" wide for Five-Patch blocks.
4. Set aside ½ yd. to sew with double chain
fabric (B) as fast triangles. Mark a 2⅜" grid of 48
squares.

Double chain (B)

1. Cut 7 strips 2" wide for Five-Patch blocks.
2. Cut 4 strips 2" wide for Puss-in-the-Corner
blocks.
3. Set aside ½ yd. to sew with background for
fast triangles.
4. Cut 5 strips 3½" wide for second border.

Single chain (C)

1. Cut 1 strip 3½" wide. Cut into 12 squares
3½".
2. Cut 3 strips 2" wide. Cut into 48 squares 2".
3. Cut 5 strips 2" wide for Five-Patch blocks.
4. Cut 5 strips 2" wide for first border.
5. Cut 6 strips 2½" wide for binding.

PIECING AND ASSEMBLY

1. Make 12 Variable Star blocks that look like
this:

2. Make 17 Puss-in-the-Corner blocks that
look like this:

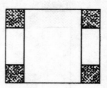

3. Make 6 Five-Patch blocks that look like
this:

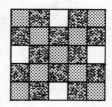

4. Follow illustration to assemble quilt.

BORDERS

1. For first border, take 2" wide strips of
single chain fabric (C) and measure off 2 strips
33½" long. Sew to top and bottom. Press.
    Piece remaining strips (on the slant) and
measure off 2 strips 50" long. Sew to long sides.
Press.
2. For second border, take 3½" wide strips of
double chain fabric (B) and measure off 2 strips
36½" long. Sew to top and bottom. Press.
    Piece remaining strips (on the slant) and
measure off 2 strips 56" long. Sew to long sides.
Press.

Fabric A ☐
Fabric B ▨
Fabric C ▨

Lap Quilt

Pieced area finishes to 46½″ by 60″.
After first border, quilt will be 49½″ by 63″.
After second border, quilt will be 55½″ by 69″.

FABRIC REQUIREMENTS

Background (A)—2½ yds.
Double chain and star (B)—2¾ yds. (2 yds. for
    piecing, ¾ yd. for second border)
Single chain (C)—2½ yds. (1¼ yds. for piecing, ½
    yd. for border, ¾ yd. for binding)
Backing—4¼ yds.

CUTTING INSTRUCTIONS

Background (A)

1. Cut 5 strips 6½″ wide. Cut into 31
rectangles 5″ by 6½″.
2. Cut 3 strips 3½″ wide.
3. Cut 4 strips 2″ wide for Five-Patch blocks.
4. Set aside ¾ yd. for fast triangles. Mark a
2⅜″ grid of 80 squares.

Double chain (B)

1. Cut 12 strips 2″ wide for Five-Patch
blocks.
2. Cut 6 strips 2″ wide for Puss-in-the-Corner
blocks.
3. Set aside ¾ yd. to sew with background
fabric (A) for fast triangles.
4. Cut 7 strips 3½″ wide for second border.

Single chain (C)

1. Cut 9 strips 2″ wide for Five-Patch blocks.
2. Cut 2 strips 3½″ wide. Cut into 20 squares
3½″.
3. Cut 5 strips 2″ wide. Cut into 80 squares 2″.
4. Cut 6 strips 2″ wide for first border.
5. Cut 8 strips 2½″ wide for binding.

PIECING AND ASSEMBLY

1. Make 20 Variable Star blocks that look like
this:

2. Make 12 Five-Patch blocks that look like
this:

HINT: Make 2 sets of row 1, 2 of row 2, and only
1 of row 3.

3. Make 31 Puss-in-the-Corner blocks that
look like this:

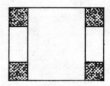

4. Follow illustration to assemble quilt.

BORDERS

1. For first border, piece 2″ wide strips of
single chain fabric (C) (on the slant). Measure off
2 strips 47″ long and sew to top and bottom.
Press.
    Measure off 2 strips 63½″ long, and sew to
long sides. Press.
2. For second border, piece 3½″ wide strips of
double chain fabric (B) (on the slant). Measure off
2 strips 50″ long and sew to top and bottom.
Press.
    Measure off 2 strips 69½″ long and sew to
long sides. Press.

Album quilt in miniature by Trudie Hughes, 1988, 20" square. This size is just right for gift-giving.

Album quilt by Trudie Hughes, 1988, 53-1/2" by 70-1/2". Fabrics and signatures collected from friends would make a wonderful scrap quilt to cherish.

Album quilt by Trudie Hughes, 1988, 37-3/4" by 46-1/4". In pastels, this quilt would be a treasure for any baby.

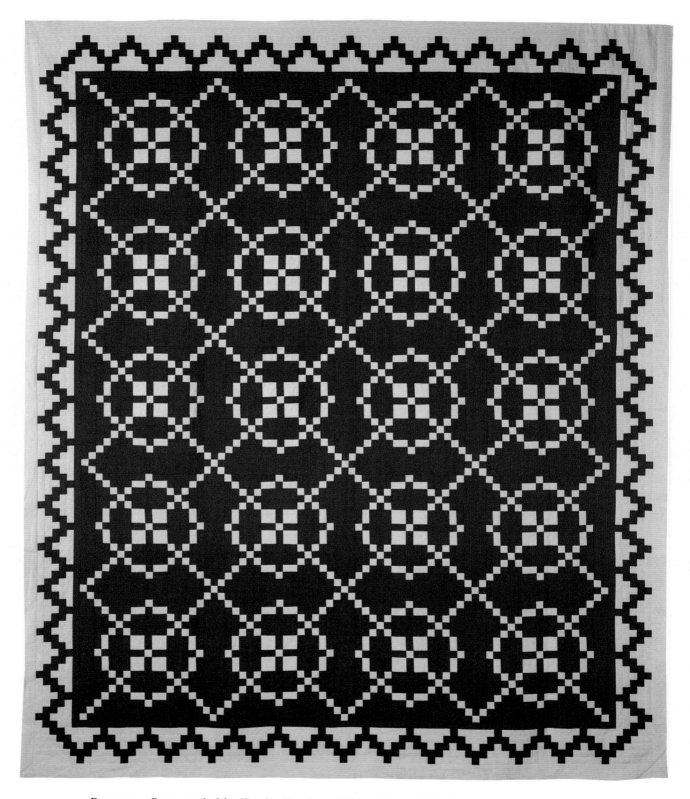

Burgoyne Surrounded by Trudie Hughes, 1988, 89" by 107". Graphic in navy and white, though traditional in design, this quilt attracts attention.

Burgoyne Surrounded by Trudie Hughes, 1988, 53" by 71". This wall hanging or lap quilt will please red and white quilt lovers.

Jacob's Elevator by Trudie Hughes, 1988, 55" by 79". Dynamic colors make for a striking lap quilt.

Jacob's Elevator by Trudie Hughes, 1988, 84" by 108". This quilt is just right for using those bold prints.

Evening in Ireland by Trudie Hughes, 1988, 99" by 112-1/2". The pieced border adds spice to this pastel version.

Evening in Ireland by Trudie Hughes, 1988, 55-1/2" by 69." Red, white, and blue make an appealing combination.

Evening in Ireland by Trudie Hughes, 1988, 42" by 55-1/2". A darker background gives this peach and green quilt a very different look.

Evening in Ireland by Trudie Hughes and Cheryl Chaveriat, 1988, 83-1/2" by 97".
For those who love blue, this full-size quilt is a winner.

*Woven Hearts by Trudie Hughes, 1988, 48-1/2" by 58-1/2".
In dramatic purples, this lap quilt also gives you room for
interesting quilting.*

*Woven Hearts by Trudie Hughes, 1988,
35-1/2" by 45-1/2". Red and pink make this
a special Valentine quilt.*

Woven Hearts by Trudie Hughes, 1988, 79" by 109". This quilt is perfect for a little girl's room.

Woven Hearts by Trudie Hughes, 1988, 49" by 55". This quilt, with its pieced border, would add interest to any wall.

Road to St. Louis by Trudie Hughes, 1988, 48-3/4" by 61". This scrap quilt is sure to be a winner. The red print enhances all the other fabrics in the quilt.

Road to St. Louis by Trudie Hughes, 1988, 78" by 102". Lively prints are surrounded by a charming brown print.

Shortcut to School by Trudie Hughes, 1988, 36" by 50". Done in pastels, this quilt features a wonderful design.

Shortcut to School by Trudie Hughes, 1988, 83" by 104". A strong combination of black and pink enhances the design.

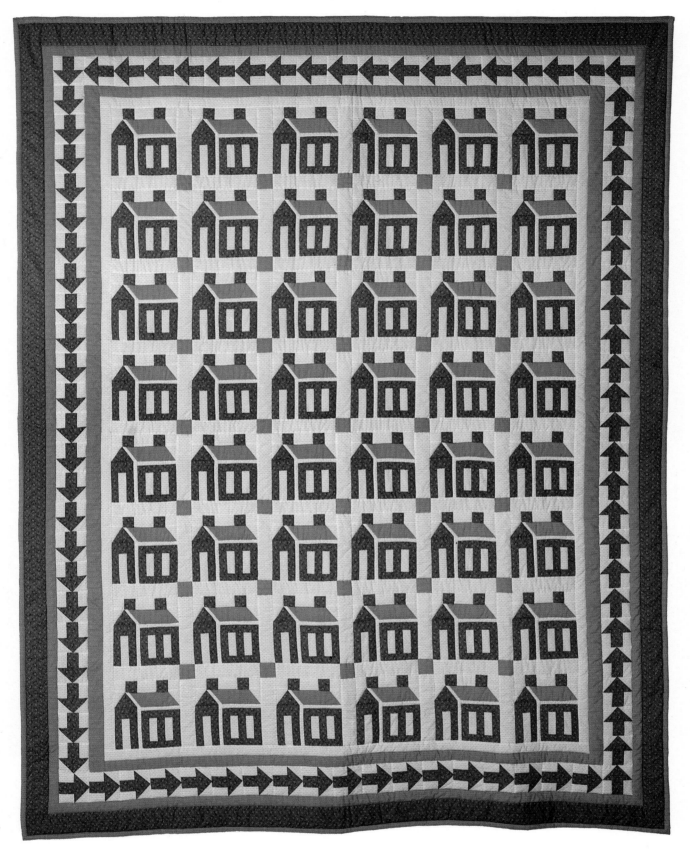

This Way to My House by Trudie Hughes, 1988, 85" by 109". The pieced border of arrows makes for fun piecing of this blue, pink, and white quilt.

*This Way to My House by Trudie Hughes, 1988, 45"
by 57". The making of this traditional red and white
quilt goes so fast, you might want to try the border
of arrows.*

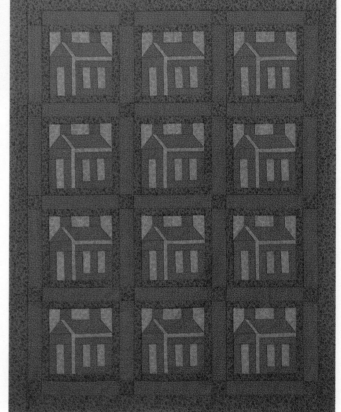

*This Way to My House by Trudie Hughes, 1988,
45-1/2" by 60". A small frame of accent fabric is
added around each house block. The pieced border
is eliminated in this alternate setting.*

Feathered Star by Trudie Hughes, 1988, 81" by 108". This quilt, which she hand quilted herself, is the author's favorite.

Feathered Star by Trudie Hughes, 1988, 51" by 63". A sawtooth border surrounds this black and gray combination.

Fabric A
Fabric B
Fabric C

Large Quilt

Pieced area finishes to 73½" by 87".
After first border, quilt will be 76½" by 90".
After second border, quilt will be 81" by 94½".

FABRIC REQUIREMENTS

Background (A)—6½ yds. (4 yds. for piecing, 1½ yds. for 2nd and 4th borders, 1 yd. for pieced border)

Double chain and star (B)—7 yds. (3¼ yds. for piecing, 1½ yds. for first and last borders, 1 yd. for binding, 1¼ yds. for pieced border)

Single chain (C)—2¾ yds. (2 yds. for piecing, ¾ yd. for pieced border)

Backing—10 yds.

CUTTING INSTRUCTIONS

Background (A)

1. Cut 9 strips 6½" wide. Cut into 71 rectangles 5" by 6½".
2. Cut 7 strips 3½" wide.
3. Cut 7 strips 2" wide for five patches.
4. Set aside 1 yd. for fast triangles. Mark a 2⅜" grid of 168 squares. (It would be helpful to handle these in several sections.)
5. Cut 18 strips 2¾" wide for second and fourth borders.

For pieced border:

Cut 8 strips 3⅜" wide. Cut into 86 squares 3⅜". Cut with an X to yield 344 quarter-square triangles.

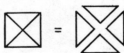

Double chain (B)

1. Cut 19 strips 2" wide for five patches.
2. Cut 14 strips 2" wide for Puss-in-the-Corner blocks.
3. Set aside 1 yd. for fast triangles.
4. Cut 8 strips 2" wide for first border.
5. Cut 10 strips 3" wide for last border.
6. Cut 11 strips 2½" wide for binding.

For pieced border:

Cut 18 strips 2" wide.

Single chain (C)

1. Cut 14 strips 2" wide for five patches.
2. Cut 4 strips 3½" wide. Cut into 42 squares 3½".
3. Cut 9 strips 2" wide. Cut these into 168 squares 2".

For pieced border:

Cut 9 strips 2" wide.

PIECING AND ASSEMBLY

1. Make 42 Variable Star blocks that look like this:

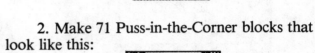

2. Make 71 Puss-in-the-Corner blocks that look like this:

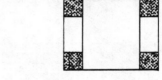

3. Make 30 Five-Patch blocks that look like this:

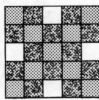

HINT: Make 3 strips of row 1, 3 strips of row 2, and 2 strips of row 3.

4. Follow illustration to assemble quilt.

BORDERS

1. For first border, piece 2" wide strips of double chain fabric (B) (on the slant). Measure off 2 strips 74" long and sew to top and bottom. Press.
Measure off 2 strips 90½" long and sew to long sides. Press.
2. For second border, piece 2¾" wide strips of background fabric (A). Measure off 2 strips 77" long and sew to top and bottom. Press.
Measure off 2 strips 95" long and sew to long sides. Press.

Large Quilt with Pieced Border

After pieced border, quilt will be 89½″ by 103″.
After fourth border, quilt will be 94″ by 107½″.
After last border, quilt will be 99″ by 112½″.

Fabric A
Fabric B
Fabric C

CREATIVE OPTION

Marie Zimmer made this quilt with a wonderful pieced border, and I couldn't help adapting her idea to my large quilt. However, it does increase the size of the quilt dramatically.

This pieced border looks like Seminole piecing, but I found that that type of piecing wasn't the best way to handle such a long border. The bias edge makes the border too stretchy. Quarter-square triangles placed at the ends of units instead of squares make the border more stable for piecing and sewing.

1. Make 9 sets of strips that look like this:

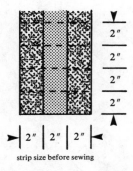

2″
2″
2″
2″

▶|2″|2″|2″|◀

strip size before sewing

Press all seams toward double chain fabric (B). Cut every 2″. Sew a quarter-square triangle onto ends of 148 of these units.

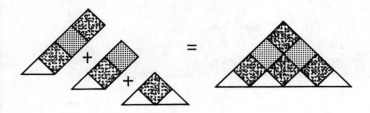

2. Make 4 fill-in units that look like this:

3. Make 2 border strips by sewing together 34 "pieced border" units.

Add a fill-in unit to right end of each strip. Sew to top and bottom of quilt. Press.

4. Make 2 border strips by sewing together 40 "pieced border" units.

Add a fill-in unit to right end of each strip. Sew to long sides of quilt. Press.

5. Piece 4 corner units that look like this:

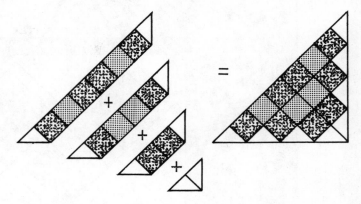

Sew onto 4 corners of quilt.

6. After pieced border is added to quilt, piece remaining 2¾″ wide strips of background fabric (A) for fourth border. Measure off 2 strips 90″ long and sew to top and bottom. Press. Measure off 2 strips 108″ long and sew to long sides. Press.

7. Piece 3″ wide strips of double chain fabric (B) (on the slant) and measure off 2 strips 94½″ long. Sew to top and bottom. Press.

Measure off 2 strips 113″ long and sew to long sides. Press.

WOVEN HEARTS

Fabric A
Fabric B
Fabric C

Crib Quilt or Wall Hanging

18 Heart blocks, 7" finished
Pieced area finishes to 29½" by 39½".
After first border, quilt will be 37" by 43".
After pieced border, quilt will be 43" by 49".
After last border, quilt will be 49" by 55".

This charming quilt was designed by Ruth Hartung. I spotted it immediately as a candidate for my "Speedies" technique. This quilt is offered in three sizes.

FABRIC REQUIREMENTS

Background (A)—2 yds. (1½ yds. for piecing, ½ yd. for pieced border)

Heart fabric (B)—2¼ yds. (½ yd. for piecing, ½ yd. for pieced border, 1¼ yd. for first and last borders)

Heart fabric (C)—1¾ yds. (½ yd. for piecing, ½ yd. for pieced border, ¾ yd. for binding)

Backing—3½ yds. (pieced crosswise)

CUTTING INSTRUCTIONS

Background (A)

1. Cut 1 strip 11¼" wide. Cut into 3 squares 11¼". Cut these with an X to yield 10 quarter-square triangles. It will be helpful to notch these setting triangles on both short sides at 7½".

2. Cut 2 squares 8". Cut these diagonally once for corners.

3. Cut 2 strips 1⅞" wide. Cut into 36 squares 1⅞". Cut these diagonally to yield 72 half-square triangles. It will be helpful to nub these at 1½".

4. Cut 2 strips 2½" wide. Cut into 18 squares 2½".

5. Cut 14 strips 1½" wide. Cut into 36 lengths 5½" long and 36 lengths 7½" long for borders around hearts.

For pieced border:

1. Cut 2 strips 2⅝" wide. Cut into 26 squares 2⅝". Cut these squares with an X to yield 104 quarter-square triangles.

2. Cut 3 strips 1½" wide. Cut into 52 squares 1½" and 4 rectangles 1½" by 2½".

3. Cut 2 squares 2¼". Cut these diagonally for corners of pieced border.

4. Cut 2 squares 4⅛". Cut these with an X to yield units found in center of each side of pieced border.

Heart fabric (B)

1. Cut 5 strips 1½" wide for nine patches.

2. Cut 2 strips 3½" wide. Cut into 18 rectangles 2½" by 3½". Using 1" Speedy on Rotary Mate™, cut 2 corners off 1 of long sides.

3. Cut 2 strips 2¼" wide for first border. These are added to short sides.

4. Cut 2 strips 4¼" wide for first border. These are added to long sides.

5. Cut 7 strips 3½" wide for last border.

For pieced border:

1. Cut 8 strips 1½" wide. Cut into 112 trapezoids, cutting back at 2⅞". You will need 56 with points going in 1 direction and 56 with points going in opposite direction.

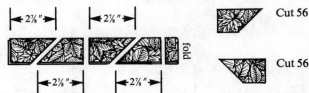

2. Cut 1 strip 1½" wide into 4 "decapitated triangles," cutting back at 5¼". (See page 11 for more information on cutting "decapitated triangles.")

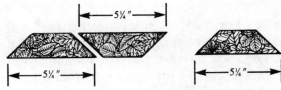

Heart fabric (C)

1. Cut 4 strips 1½" wide for nine patches.
2. Cut 2 strips 3½" wide. Cut into 18 rectangles 2½" by 3½". Using 1" Speedy on Rotary Mate™, cut 2 corners off 1 long side.

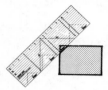

3. Cut 7 strips 2½" wide for binding.

For pieced border:

1. Cut 7 strips 1½" wide. Cut these into 104 trapezoids, cutting back at 2⅞". You will need 52 with points going in 1 direction and 52 with points going opposite direction. Cut the same as heart fabric (B).

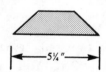

2. Cut 1 strip 1½" wide into 4 "decapitated triangles," cutting back at 5¼". Cut the same as heart fabric (B).

PIECING AND ASSEMBLY

1. Make 3 sets of strips that look like this:

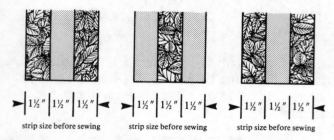

Place rows 1 and 2 right sides together and make 18 cuts at 1½". Sew in pairs. With row 3, make 18 cuts at 1½". Sew to rows 1 and 2, making 18 nine patches. (See page 12 for more information on making nine patches.)

Make 18

2. Sew a background triangle onto each side of rectangles where you used the Speedy to cut off corners.

3. Assemble blocks to look like this:

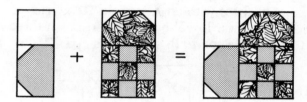

Make 18 hearts.

4. Border hearts with 1½" wide border strips, sewing on short sides first. Press, then sew on long sides. Press.
5. Following illustration, sew blocks into rows, adding setting triangles onto ends of rows. Match corner and notch of setting triangle with block. Sew with triangle as the underneath layer.

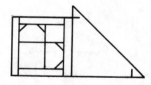

6. Join rows, making sure that setting triangles intersect at ¼" on ends, resulting in a straight edge along outside of quilt.

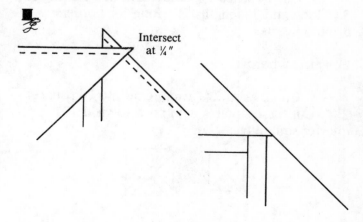

Intersect at ¼"

7. Add corners. Corner triangles will be too large, but sew them on anyway. After pressing, use your plastic triangle to trim triangles to match quilt.

8. After pieced area is complete, add first border. Take 2¼" wide strips and measure off 2 strips 30" long. Sew to top and bottom. Press.

Take 4¼" wide strips and measure off 2 strips 43½" long. Sew to long sides. Press. If fabric is not wide enough, you may have to cut 1 more strip and piece long borders.

HINT: These 2 widths of strips are necessary to make pieced border mathematically compatible.

CREATIVE OPTION

After adding first border, you may add a pieced border.

1. Make 52 units that resemble the attic windows pattern:

2. Make 52 trapezoid units that look like this:

Make 52 trapezoid units that look like this:

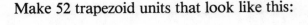

3. Make 4 corner units that look like this:

4. After you have made all parts, make 2 border strips that look like this:

Sew to short sides.

5. Make 2 border strips that look like this:

Sew to long sides.

6. Add corner units.

7. After pieced border is sewn to quilt, add last border.

Take 3½" wide strips of heart fabric (B) and measure off 2 strips 43½" long. Sew to top and bottom of quilt. Press. If fabric is not wide enough, you may have to cut 1 more strip and piece these together.

Piece 3 remaining strips (on the slant) and measure off 2 strips 55½" long. Sew to long sides. Press.

Lap Quilt

In this variation, there are just two more hearts than the crib size and additional room for you to quilt something special.

20 pieced hearts
Pieced area finishes to 39½" by 49½".
After first border, quilt will be 41½" by 51½".
After second border, quilt will be 48½" by 58½".

Fabric A
Fabric B
Fabric C

FABRIC REQUIREMENTS

Background (A)—2½ yds.
Heart fabric (B)—1¾ yds. (⅝ yd. for piecing,
    ½ yd. for first border, ⅝ yd. for binding)
Heart fabric (C)—½ yd.
Last border fabric—¾ yd.
Backing—3¼ yds. (pieced crosswise)

CUTTING INSTRUCTIONS

Background (A)

1. Cut 3 strips 7½" wide. Cut into 11 squares 7½".
2. Cut 2 strips 11¼" wide. Cut into 5 squares 11¼". Cut these with an X to yield 18 quarter-square triangles. It would be helpful to notch these setting triangles at 7½" on each of the short sides.

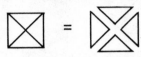

3. Cut 2 strips 1⅞" wide. Cut into 40 squares 1⅞". Cut these diagonally to yield 80 half-square triangles. It would be helpful to nub these at 1½".

4. Cut 2 strips 2½" wide. Cut into 20 squares 2½".
5. Cut 16 strips 1½" wide. Cut into 40 lengths 5½" long and 40 lengths 7½" long for borders around heart blocks.

Heart fabric (B)

1. Cut 5 strips 1½" wide for nine patches.
2. Cut 2 strips 3½" wide. Cut into 20 rectangles 2½" by 3½". Using 1" Speedy on Rotary Mate™, cut 2 corners off 1 long side.

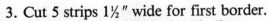

3. Cut 5 strips 1½" wide for first border.
4. Cut 6 strips 2½" wide for binding.

Heart fabric (C)

1. Cut 4 strips 1½" wide for nine patches.
2. Cut 2 strips 3½" wide. Cut into 20 rectangles 2½" by 3½". Using 1" Speedy on Rotary Mate™ cut 2 corners off 1 long side. See step 2 under Heart fabric (B).

Last border fabric

Cut 5 strips 4" wide.

PIECING AND ASSEMBLY

1. Make 3 sets of strips that look like this:

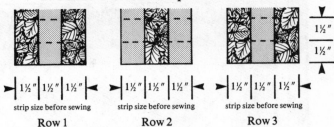

Place row 1 and row 2 right sides together and cut every 1½". Sew in pairs. With row 3, cut every 1½". Sew to pair. Make 20 nine patches. (See page 12 for more information on how to make nine patches.)

2. Sew a background triangle onto each side of rectangles where you used the Speedy to cut off corners.

3. Assemble 20 heart blocks that look like this:

4. Border hearts with 1½" border strips of background, sewing on short sides first. Press, then sew on long sides. Press.

5. Following illustration, sew heart blocks into rows with 7½" squares of background, adding setting triangles onto ends of rows. Match corner and notch of setting triangle with block. Sew with triangle as the underneath layer.

6. Join rows, making sure seams intersect at ¼" on outside edges.

7. Make each of the 4 corners from 2 setting triangles.

8. After pieced area is complete, add first border. With 1½" wide strips of heart fabric (B), measure off 2 strips 40" long and sew to top and bottom. Press.

Piece remaining strips (on the slant) and measure off 2 strips 52" long. Sew to long sides. Press.

9. Take 4" wide strips of last border fabric and measure off 2 strips 42" long. Sew to top and bottom. Press.

Piece remaining strips (on the slant) and measure off 2 strips 59" long and sew to long sides. Press.

Fabric A ▭   Fabric B ▨   Fabric C ▢

Large Quilt

39 pieced heart blocks, 10½" finished
Pieced area finishes to 60" by 90".
After first border, quilt will be 66" by 96".
After pieced border, quilt will be 72" by 102".
After third border, quilt will be 75" by 105".
After last border, quilt will be 79" by 109".

FABRIC REQUIREMENTS

Background (A)—6 yds. (4½ yds. for piecing, ¾ yd. for pieced border, ¾ yd. for third border)
Heart fabric (B)—4¼ yds. (1¼ yds for piecing, 2¼ yds. for first and last border, ¾ yd. for pieced border)
Heart fabric (C)—1¾ yds. (1¼ yds. for piecing, ½ yd. for pieced border)
Binding—1 yd.
Backing—6½ yds.

CUTTING INSTRUCTIONS

Background (A)

1. Cut 2 strips 16¼" wide. Cut into 4 squares 16¼". Cut these with an X to yield 16 quarter-square triangles. It would be helpful to notch these setting triangles at 11" on each short side.

2. Cut 2 squares 11". Cut these diagonally once for corners.

3. Cut 5 strips 2⅜" wide. Cut these into 78 squares 2⅜". Cut these diagonally to yield 156 half-square triangles. It would be helpful to nub these at 2".

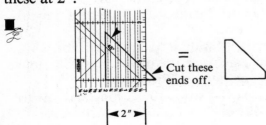

= Cut these ends off.

4. Cut 4 strips 3½" wide. Cut these into 39 squares 3½".

5. Cut 42 strips 2" wide. Cut into 78 lengths 8" long and 78 lengths 11" long for borders around hearts.

6. Cut 10 strips 2" wide for third border.

For pieced border:

1. Cut 3 strips 4¼" wide. Cut into 27 squares 4¼". Cut these squares with an X to yield 108 quarter-square triangles.

2. Cut 4 squares 3½" for corners.

Heart fabric (B)

1. Cut 5 strips 3½" wide. Cut into 39 rectangles 5" by 3½". Using 1½" Speedy on Rotary Mate™, cut 2 corners off 1 long side.

2. Cut 10 strips 2" wide for nine patches.
3. Cut 10 strips 3¾" wide for first border.
4. Cut 10 strips 2½" wide for last border.

For pieced border:

Cut 6 strips 3⅞" wide. Cut these into 54 squares 3⅞". Cut these diagonally to yield 108 half-square triangles.

Heart fabric (C)

1. Cut 5 strips 3½" wide. Cut into 39 rectangles 5" by 3½". Using 1½" Speedy on Rotary Mate™, cut 2 corners off 1 long side.
2. Cut 8 strips 2" wide for nine patches.

For pieced border:

Cut 3 strips 4¼" wide. Cut into 27 squares 4¼". Cut these with an X to yield 108 quarter-square triangles.

Binding

Cut 10 strips 2½" wide.

PIECING AND ASSEMBLY

1. Make 2 sets of each of following strips:

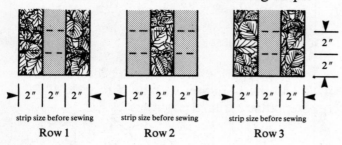

strip size before sewing	strip size before sewing	strip size before sewing
Row 1	Row 2	Row 3

Place rows 1 and 2 right sides together and cut every 2". Sew in pairs.

Cut row 3 every 2". Sew onto pairs of rows 1 and 2. Make 39 nine patches. (See page 12 for more information on how to make nine patches.)

2. Sew a background triangle onto each side of rectangles where you used the Speedy to cut off corners.

3. Assemble blocks to look like this:

Make 39 pieced hearts.

4. Border hearts with 2" border strips, sewing on short sides first. Press. Sew on long sides. Press.

5. Following illustration, sew blocks into rows, adding setting triangles onto ends of rows. Match corner and notch of setting triangle with blocks. Sew with triangle as the underneath layer.

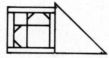

6. Join rows, making sure that setting triangles intersect at ¼" on ends, resulting in a straight edge along outside of quilt.

7. Add corners. Corner triangles will be too large, but sew them on anyway. After pressing, use your plastic triangle to clean up corners.

8. Piece 3¾" wide strips of heart fabric (B) (on the slant) and measure off 2 strips 60½" long. Sew to top and bottom. Press.

Measure off 2 strips 96½" long and sew to long sides. Press.

CREATIVE OPTION

After first border, you may add a pieced border. This pieced border is made from units that look like this:

1. Sew quarter-square triangles of background fabric (A) and heart fabric (C) together. Make 54 A units that look like this:

Make 54 B units that look like this:

2. Sew a half-square triangle of heart fabric (B) to these:

3. Sew 2 strips of 11 A units and 2 strips of 11 B units. Sew A unit strips to B unit strips. Sew to top and bottom of quilt. Press.

4. Sew 2 strips of 16 A units and 2 strips of 16 B units. Sew A unit strips to B unit strips. Sew to long sides of quilt. Press.

5. Piece 2" wide strips of background fabric (A) (on the slant) and measure off 2 strips 72½" long. Sew to top and bottom. Press.

Measure off 2 strips 105½" long and sew to long sides. Press.

6. Piece 2½" wide strips of heart fabric (B) (on the slant) and measure off 2 strips 75½" long. Sew to top and bottom. Press.

Measure off 2 strips 109½" long and sew to long sides. Press.

ROAD TO ST. LOUIS

Lap Quilt

Fabric A ▢
Fabric B ▨

Pieced area finishes to 36″ by 48″.
After first border, quilt will be 38½″ by 51″.
After pieced border, quilt will be 42¾″ by 55¼″.
After last border, quilt will be 48¾″ by 61″.

While in St. Louis to teach, I saw many great quilts. One of these belonged to Joyce Mottern, who generously agreed to let me work up her design for this book. Hers is a simple design and perfect for the rotary cutter. The only change I made from her original design was a redrafting of the pieced border to eliminate the use of templates.

FABRIC REQUIREMENTS

Background (A)—1¼ yds. (¾ yd. for piecing, ½ yd. for pieced border)
Main (B)—2 yds. (¾ yd. for piecing, ½ yd. for pieced border, ¾ yd. for first and last borders)
Assorted fabrics (C)—384 squares 2″.
Binding—¾ yd.
Backing—3¾ yd.

CUTTING INSTRUCTIONS

Background (A)

1. Cut 2 strips 7¼″ wide. Cut into 9 squares 7¼″. Cut these with an X to yield 34 quarter-square triangles.

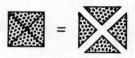

2. Cut 2 strips 3⅞″ wide. Cut into 14 squares 3⅞″. Cut these diagonally to yield 28 half-square triangles.

For pieced border:

1. Cut 4 strips 3⅜″ wide. Cut these into 43 squares 3⅜″. Cut these with an X to yield 172 quarter-square triangles.

2. Cut 4 squares 2″ wide. Cut these diagonally to yield 8 half-square triangles.

Main fabric (B)

1. Cut 3 strips 7¼″ wide. Cut into 12 squares 7¼″. Cut these squares with an X to yield 48 quarter-square triangles.

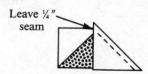

2. Cut 2 strips 2″ wide for top and bottom of first border.

3. Cut 3 strips 1¾″ wide for sides of first border.

4. Cut 6 strips 3½″ wide for last border.

For pieced border:

Cut 5 strips 2″ wide. Cut into 88 squares 2″.

Binding

Cut 7 strips 2½″ wide.

PIECING AND ASSEMBLY

1. Make 14 Flying Geese units that look like this:

HINT: When piecing these, set first triangle in corner and sew.

When second triangle is added, set in corner, but be sure that seams intersect at ¼″.

Leave ¼″ seam

Results should be a straight edge with a ¼″ seam allowance remaining.

2. Make 17 quarter-square triangle units that look like this:

3. Make 18 sixteen patches of assorted fabrics (C) that look like this:

4. Make 10 half blocks of assorted fabrics (C) that look like this:

5. Make 4 Four Patches of assorted fabrics (C) that look like this:

6. Following illustration, assemble quilt in rows.

7. After pieced area is completed, add first border. Take the 2″ wide strips of main fabric (B) and measure off 2 strips 36½″ long. Sew to top and bottom. Press.

Piece 1½″ wide strips of main fabric (B) (on the slant) and measure off 2 strips 51½″ long and sew to long sides.

CREATIVE OPTION

After the first border, a pieced border may be added.

1. Make 78 units that have a quarter-square triangle of background fabric (A) added to each side of a small square. They should look like this:

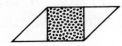

Make 2 units that look like this:

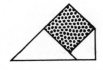

Make 2 units that look like this:

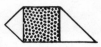

Make 2 units that look like this:

2. Sew 2 border strips that look like this, referring to diagram on page 69 for complete segments:

NOTE: The beginning and end of each strip has a small half-square triangle. Sew these to top and bottom of quilt.

3. Sew 2 border strips that look like this, referring to diagram on page 69 for complete segments:

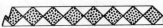

Sew to long sides of quilt.

4. Make 4 corner units that look like this:

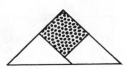

5. For last border, take 3″ wide strips of main fabric (B) and measure off 2 strips 43¼″ long and sew to top and bottom. Press.

Piece remaining strips and measure off 2 strips 61½″ long and sew to long sides. Press.

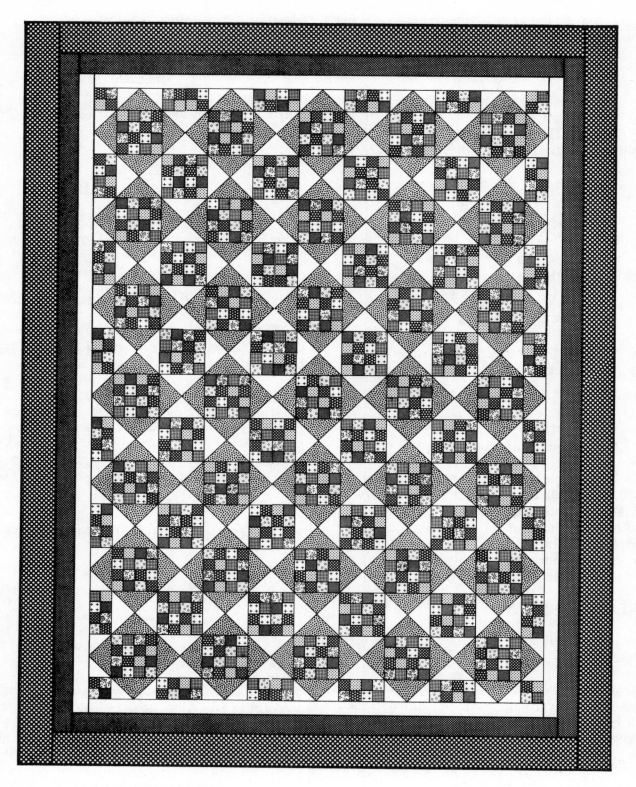

Large Quilt

Pieced area finishes to 60″ by 84″.
After first border, quilt will be 64″ by 88″.
After second border, quilt will be 70″ by 94″.
After last border, quilt will be 78″ by 102″.

Fabric A
Fabric B

FABRIC REQUIREMENTS

Background (A)—2½ yds. (1¾ yds. for piecing, ¾ yd. for first border)
Main (B)—1⅛ yds.
Assorted fabrics (C)—1120 squares 2".
Second border—1 yd.
Last border—1½ yds.
Binding—1 yd.
Backing—6 yds.

CUTTING INSTRUCTIONS

Background (A)

1. Cut 6 strips 7¼" wide. Cut into 29 squares 7¼". Cut these with an **X** to yield 116 quarter-square triangles.

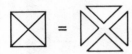

2. Cut 3 strips 3⅞" wide. Cut into 24 squares 3⅞". Cut these diagonally to yield 48 half-square triangles.

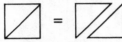

3. Cut 8 strips 2½" wide for first border.

Main fabric (B)

Cut 7 strips 7¼" wide. Cut into 35 squares 7¼". Cut these squares with an **X** to yield 140 quarter-square triangles.

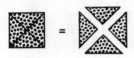

Second border

Cut 9 strips 3½" wide.

Last border

Cut 9 strips 4½" wide.

Binding

Cut 10 strips 2½" wide.

PIECING AND ASSEMBLY

1. Make 24 Flying Geese units that look like this:

HINT: When piecing these, set first triangle in corner and sew.

When second triangle is added, set in corner, but be sure that seams intersect at ¼".

Results should be a straight edge with a ¼" seam allowance remaining.

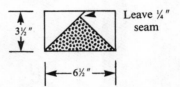

2. Make 58 quarter-square triangle units that look like this:

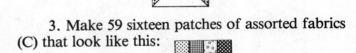

3. Make 59 sixteen patches of assorted fabrics (C) that look like this:

4. Make 20 half blocks of assorted fabrics (C) that look like this:

5. Make 4 Four Patches of assorted fabrics (C) that look like this:

6. Following illustration, assemble quilt in rows.

7. After pieced area is completed, add first border. Piece 2½" wide strips of background fabric (A) (on the slant) and measure off 2 strips 60½" long and sew to top and bottom. Press. Measure off 2 strips 88½" long and sew to long sides. Press.

8. Piece 3½" wide strips of second border fabric (on the slant) and measure off 2 strips 64½" long. Sew to top and bottom. Press. Measure off 2 strips 94½" long and sew to long sides. Press.

9. Piece 4½" wide strips of last border fabric. Measure off 2 strips 70½" long and sew to top and bottom. Press. Measure off 2 strips 102½" long and sew to long sides. Press.

SHORTCUT TO SCHOOL

Joan Padgett and Lynette Chiles of Tomorrow's Heirlooms came out with a wonderful pattern called Shortcut to School. Their version has an appliqued schoolhouse in the center. I went wild for the design because it has trapezoids in it. Such simple ingredients make such a smashing quilt.

Crib Quilt

Pieced area finishes to 32″ by 46″.
After last border, quilt will be 36″ by 50″.

Fabric A	☐
Fabric B	▨
Fabric C	▦
Fabric D	■

FABRIC REQUIREMENTS

Light fabric (A)—1 yd.
Main large print (B)—1 yd.
Accent (C)—½ yd.
Accent (D)—½ yd.
Last border—½ yd.
Binding—½ yd.
Backing—1⅝ yds.

CUTTING INSTRUCTIONS

Light (A)

1. Cut 6 strips 2½″ wide. With strips folded in half, right sides together, cut trapezoids, measuring cuts at 3⅞″ intervals.

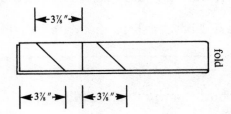

You will need 48 trapezoids with points going in 1 direction and 48 trapezoids with points going in opposite direction. (See page 10 for more information on cutting trapezoids.)

Make 48   Make 48

2. Cut 4 strips 2½″ wide. Cut 6 "decapitated triangles," cutting back at 15¼," and cut 8 "decapitated triangles," cutting back at 10¼″. (See page 11 for more information on cutting "decapitated triangles.")

Make 6

←————— 15¼″ —————→

Make 8

←——— 10¼″ ———→

Main large print (B)

1. Cut 4 strips 2⅞″ wide. Cut into 48 squares 2⅞″. Cut these squares diagonally to yield 96 half-square triangles.

2. Cut 8 strips 1½″ wide for nine patches.
3. Cut 1 strip 5¼″ wide. Cut this into 3 squares 5¼″. Cut these squares with an X to yield 10 quarter-square triangles.

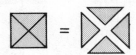

Accent (C)

1. Cut 3 strips 2½″ wide for large Four Patches.
2. Cut 3 strips 1½″ wide for nine patches.

Accent (D)

1. Cut 3 strips 2½″ wide for large Four Patches.
2. Cut 3 strips 1½″ wide for nine patches.

Last border

Cut 5 strips 2½″ wide.

Binding

Cut 5 strips 2½″ wide.

PIECING AND ASSEMBLY

1. For nine patches, make 1 of each of the following sets of strips:

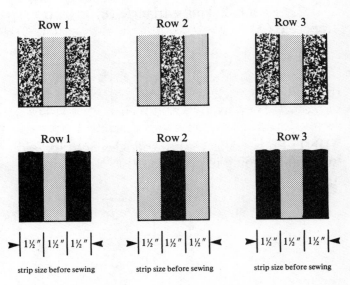

Row 1   Row 2   Row 3

←|1½″|1½″|1½″|→   ►|1½″|1½″|1½″|◄   ►|1½″|1½″|1½″|◄

strip size before sewing   strip size before sewing   strip size before sewing

Cut strips every 1½". Make 12 nine patches of each combination. (See page 12 for more information on making nine patches.)

Make 12   Make 12

2. Make 3 sets of strips for large Four Patches that look like this:

►|2½"|2½"|◄
strip size before sewing

Place 2 of these strips right sides together and cut every 2½". Sew 15 of these pairs to look like this:

Take remaining strip and cut every 2½" to make 16 units that look like this:

You will need 2 loose squares 2½" of each accent fabric for corners of quilt.

3. Sew a half-square triangle (B) to each trapezoid (A).

   =

HINT: Press seams toward triangles on trapezoids with points going upper right.

Press seams toward trapezoids with points going upper left.

This hint will be helpful when sewing 2 trapezoids together, as seams will be going opposite directions.

4. When all parts are made, assemble quilt in rows, following illustration. There will be wide rows and narrow rows.

5. The first border is made up of "decapitated triangles" (A) and quarter-square triangles (B).

Make 2 border strips that look like this:

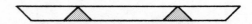

Make 2 border strips that look like this:

When adding these borders to quilt, begin and end backstitching ¼" from ends; then miter out.

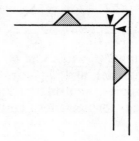

6. With 2½" wide strips of border fabric, measure off 2 strips 32½" long and sew to top and bottom. Press.

Piece remaining strips (on the slant) and measure off 2 strips 50½" long and sew to long sides of quilt. Press.

Large Quilt

Pieced area finishes to 69″ by 90″.
After last border, quilt will be 83″ by 104″.

Fabric A
Fabric B
Fabric C
Fabric D

FABRIC REQUIREMENTS

Background (A)—3 yds.
Main (B)—2⅜ yds.
Accent (C)—1½ yds.
Accent (D)—1½ yds.
Second border—1 yd.
Third border—1½ yds.
Binding—1 yd.
Backing—6¼ yds.

CUTTING INSTRUCTIONS

Background (A)

1. Cut 20 strips 3½" wide. With these strips folded in half, right sides together, cut trapezoids, measuring cuts at 5⅜". (See page 10 for more information on cutting trapezoids.)

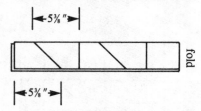

You will need 96 trapezoids with their points going in 1 direction and 96 trapezoids with points going opposite direction.

Make 96   Make 96

2. Cut 9 strips 3½" wide. Cut 10 "decapitated triangles," measuring cuts at 22¼".
Cut 8 "decapitated triangles," measuring cuts at 14¾". (See page 11 for more information on cutting "decapitated triangles.")

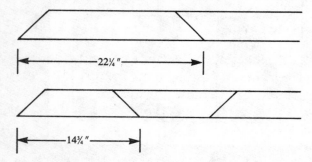

Main (B)

1. Cut 16 strips 2" wide for nine patches.
2. Cut 10 strips 3⅞" wide. Cut into 96 squares 3⅞", then cut diagonally to yield 192 half-square triangles.

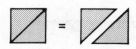

3. Cut 1 strip 7¼" wide. Cut into 4 squares 7¼". Cut these squares with an X to yield 14 quarter-square triangles.

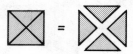

Accent (C)

1. Cut 8 strips 3½" wide for large four patches.
2. Cut 10 strips 2" wide for nine patches.

Accent (D)

1. Cut 8 strips 3½" wide for large four patches.
2. Cut 10 strips 2" wide for nine patches.

Second border

Cut 9 strips 3½" wide.

Third border

Cut 9 strips 4½" wide.

Binding

Cut 10 strips 2½" wide.

PIECING AND ASSEMBLY

1. For nine patches, make 2 of each of the following sets of strips:

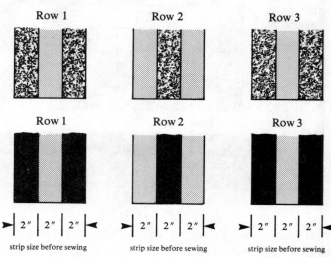

Row 1   Row 2   Row 3

Row 1   Row 2   Row 3

|← 2" | 2" | 2" →| |← 2" | 2" | 2" →| |← 2" | 2" | 2" →|

strip size before sewing   strip size before sewing   strip size before sewing

Cut every 2″. Make 24 nine patches of each combination. (See page 12 for more information on how to make nine patches.)

Make 24   Make 24

2. Make 8 sets of strips that look like this:

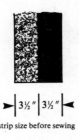

strip size before sewing

Cut every 3½″. Sew 35 pairs for large Four Patches that look this:

You will need 24 pairs of squares that look like this:

Leave 2 loose squares of each color for corners of quilt.

3. Sew a half-square triangle (B) to each trapezoid (A).

HINT: Press seams toward triangles on trapezoids with points going upper right.

Press seams toward trapezoids with points going upper left.

This hint will be helpful when sewing 2 trapezoid units together, as seams will be going in opposite directions.

4. When all parts are made, assemble quilt in rows, following illustration.
There will be wide rows and narrow rows.

5. The first border is made up of "decapitated triangles" (A) and quarter-square triangles (B).
Make 2 border strips that look like this for top and bottom:

Make a border for each side, referring to large diagram on page 44 for complete segment:

When adding borders to quilt, begin and end backstitching ¼″ from ends, then miter out.

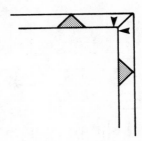

6. Piece 3½″ wide strips of second border fabric (on the slant). Measure off 2 strips 69½″ long and sew to top and bottom of quilt. Press.
Measure off 2 strips 96½″ long and sew to long sides. Press.

7. Piece 4½″ wide strips of third border fabric (on the slant) and measure off 2 strips 75½″ long. Sew to top and bottom. Press.
Measure off 2 strips 104½″ long and sew to long sides. Press.

THIS WAY TO MY HOUSE

Fabric A
Fabric B

I found house quilts discouraging to make until I was able to design this pattern without templates. Although the houses are individual blocks, the piecing is streamlined so that many houses are pieced at the same time.

My version of this quilt is traditional, with the addition of a pieced border reminiscent of my driving. Whenever I go somewhere, I seem to get lost and have to drive around and around before I find my destination.

Lap Quilt

12 houses, measuring 8½" by 9"
Pieced area finishes to 28½" by 40½".
After first border, quilt will be 31½" by 43½".
After second border, quilt will be 36" by 48".
After pieced border, quilt will be 42" by 54".
After last border, quilt will be 45" by 57".

FABRIC REQUIREMENTS

Background (A)—2¼ yds. (¾ yd. for houses, ¾ yd. for lattice and first border, ¾ yd. for pieced border)

Main (B)—3⅜ yds. (1¼ yds. for piecing, ½ yd. for pieced border, 1 yd. for second and last borders, ⅝ yd. for binding)

Backing—3 yds. (pieced crosswise)

CUTTING INSTRUCTIONS

Background (A)

1. Cut 2 strips ⅞" wide. Cut into 12 segments 5½" long.

2. Cut 4 strips 1" wide. Take 2 of these and cut into 12 segments 6" long.

3. Cut 4 strips 1½" wide.

4. Cut 2 strips 2" wide.

5. Cut 1 strip 3" wide.

6. Cut 1 strip 3" wide. With strip folded in half, cut into 12 rectangles 2¼" long. Cut these rectangles diagonally.

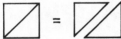

7. Cut 5 strips 2" wide. Cut into 9 strips 9" long, and 8 strips 9½" long for lattice.

8. Cut 5 strips 2" wide for first border.

For pieced border:

1. Cut 4 strips 2⅜" wide. Cut into 60 squares 2⅜". Cut these diagonally to yield 120 half-square triangles.

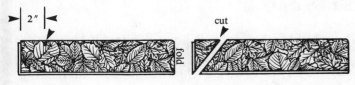

2. Cut 6 strips 1½" wide.

Main (B)

1. Cut 11 strips 1½" wide. Take 2 of these and cut into 12 segments 5½" long.

2. Cut 3 strips 2" wide. Take 1 of these and cut into 12 segments 3½" long.

3. (Peak) Cut 1 strip about ⅓₂" less than 2¾" wide. With strip folded in half, straighten left edge, then measure 2" in from top edge and make a dot.

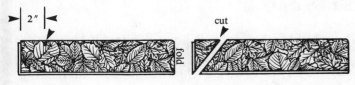

Cut from bottom left corner to this dot.

From these 2 starting points, measure off at 4" intervals and cut from dot to dot. You will need 12 of these roof sections.

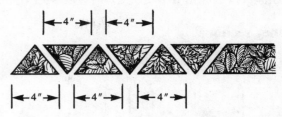

4. Cut 2 strips 2½" wide. With both strips opened up and layered, right sides up, straighten left edges. Measure in 2" from bottom edge and make a dot.

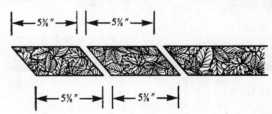

Cut from top edge to dot.

From these 2 starting points, measure off at 5⅝" intervals. Cut from dot to dot. You will need 12.

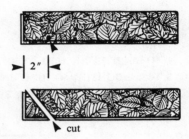

5. Cut 1 strip 2" wide. From this strip, cut 6 squares 2" for lattice corners.

6. Cut 5 strips 2¾" wide for second border.

7. Cut 6 strips 2" wide for last border.

8. Cut 7 strips 2½" wide for binding.

For pieced border:

1. Cut 2 strips 4¼" wide. Cut these into 15 squares 4¼". Cut these squares with an X to yield 60 quarter-square triangles.

2. Cut 3 strips 1½" wide.

3. Cut border strips as specified on page 83, step 2 of borders.

PIECING AND ASSEMBLY

This quilt can be pieced more efficiently if the house is broken down into 4 basic sections.

Chimney sections

Make 1 set of strips that look like this:

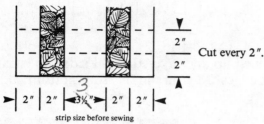

Cut every 2″.

strip size before sewing

Roof sections

1. Sew a ⅞″ background strip to left side of parallelogram. Press and trim to match edges. Sew triangle to right side of parallelogram.

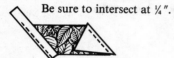

Be sure to intersect at ¼″.

2. Add triangle of background fabric (A) to left side of peak. Sew units together.

Door section

1. Sew 2 set-ups that look like this:

4½″   Cut every 4½″.

1½″ 1½″ 1½″

strip size before sewing

2. Sew a 2″ by 3½″ main (B) rectangle to tops.
3. Add a 1″ background (A) strip to right sides.

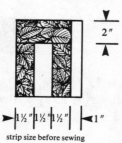

2″

1½″ 1½″ 1½″   1″

strip size before sewing

Window sections

1. Sew 1 set of strips that looks like this:

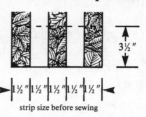

3½″

1½″ 1½″ 1½″ 1½″ 1½″

strip size before sewing

Cut into 12 segments 3½″ long.

2. Sew 2 sets of strips that look like this:

5½″

1″   1½″

strip size before sewing

Cut every 5½″ into 12 segments. Sew to top of step 1 units.

3. Sew a 5½″ segment of main fabric (B) to bottom.

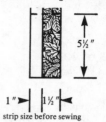

5½″

Piecing the House

1. Sew chimney section to top of roof section.
2. Sew door section to left side of window section.
3. Add roof/chimney sections to door/window sections.

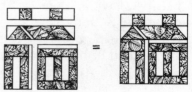

Setting the Quilt

1. Sew 4 rows of 3 houses with 9½″ long lattice pieces.
2. Sew 3 rows of 9″ lattice pieces, alternating with main 2″ squares.
3. Following illustration, assemble quilt.

Borders

1. For first border, take 2″ wide strips of background fabric (A) and measure off 2 strips 29″ long. Sew to top and bottom. Press.

Measure off 2 strips 44″ long and sew to long sides. Press. If fabric is not wide enough, you may have to cut an additional strip and piece them to get this length.

2. For second border, take 2¾″ wide strips of main fabric (B) and measure off 2 strips 32″ long. Sew to top and bottom of quilt. Press.

Piece remaining strips and measure off 2 strips 48½″ long. Sew to long sides. Press.

CREATIVE OPTION

After borders are sewed on, you may add the pieced border.

1. Sew 3 sets of strips that look like this:

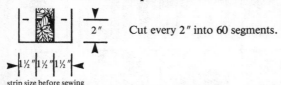

Cut every 2″ into 60 segments.

2. Sew half-square triangles of background to quarter-square triangles of main fabric.

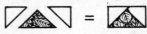

3. Make 60 arrows by sewing together pieces made in steps 1 and 2.

4. Sew 2 border strips of 12 arrows that look like this:

Sew to top and bottom.

5. Sew 2 border strips of 18 arrows, following illustration:

Sew to long sides of quilt.

6. After pieced border is sewed on, take 2″ wide strips of main fabric (B) and measure off 2 strips 42½″ long. Sew to top and bottom. Press.

Piece remaining strips (on the slant) and measure off 2 strips 57½″ long. Sew to long sides. Press.

Alternate Setting for Lap Quilt

Use accent fabric for lattice squares, border, and around each house block. Finished size is 45½″ x 60″.

FABRIC REQUIREMENTS

Background (A)—¾ yd.
Main fabric (B)—2¼ yds. (1¼ yds. for house, 1 yd. for lattice)
Accent (C)—1¼ yds. for frames, lattice squares
Backing—3 yds. (pieced crosswise)

Fabric A
Fabric B
Fabric C

CUTTING INSTRUCTIONS

Background (A)
1. See background, steps 1-6, on page 81.

Main (B)
1. See Main (B), steps 1-4, on page 81.
2. Cut 5 strips 2½″ wide. From these cut 15 lengths 11″.
3. Cut 6 strips 2½″ wide. From these cut 16 lengths 11½″.

Accent (C)
1. Cut 12 strips 1½″ wide. From each strip cut 2 lengths 9″ and 2 lengths 11½″.
2. Cut 2 strips 2½″ wide. Cut into 20 squares 2½″.
3. Cut 5 strips 3½″ wide for last border.

PIECING AND ASSEMBLY

1. Piece houses according to directions beginning on page 82.
2. Sew 9″ long strips of accent fabric to top and bottom of each house block. Press.
3. Sew 11½″ long strips of accent fabric to long sides of each house block. Press.
4. Sew 4 rows of 3 houses with 11½″ long main fabric lattice strips.
5. Sew 3 rows of 11″ long main fabric lattice strips, alternating with 2½″ accent fabric squares.
6. Add 3½″ wide borders cut from accent fabric.

Fabric A ☐   Fabric B ▨   Fabric C ▨

Large Quilt

48 houses, measuring 8½ by 9″
Pieced area finishes to 61″ by 86″.
After first border, quilt will be 64″ by 89″.
After second border, quilt will be 68″ by 92″.
After pieced border, quilt will be 76″ by 100″.
After fourth border, quilt will be 79″ by 103″.
After last border, quilt will be 85″ by 109″.

FABRIC REQUIREMENTS

Background (A)—5¾ yds. (4½ yds. for piecing and
    first border, 1¼ yds. for pieced border)
Main (B)—4½ yds. (2½ yds. for piecing, 1 yd. for
    border, 1 yd. for pieced border)
Accent (C)—3¼ yds. (1 yd. for piecing, 1¼ yds.
    for borders, 1 yd. for binding)
Backing—9¾ yds.

CUTTING INSTRUCTIONS

Background (A)

1. Cut 7 strips ⅞″ wide. Cut these into 48
segments 5½″ long.
2. Cut 7 strips 1″ wide.
3. Cut 7 strips 1″ wide. Cut into 48 segments
6″ long.
4. Cut 14 strips 1½″ wide.
5. Cut 5 strips 2″ wide.
6. Cut 3 strips 3″ wide.
7. Cut 3 strips 3″ wide. Fold these strips in
half and cut into 48 rectangles 2¼″ long. Cut these
rectangles diagonally.
8. Cut 21 strips 2½″ wide. Cut into 40 lengths
9½″ long and 42 lengths 9″ long for lattice.
9. Cut 8 strips 2″ wide for first border.

For pieced border:

1. Cut 12 strips 1¾″ wide.
2. Cut 6 strips 2⅞″ wide. Cut into 84 squares
2⅞″. Then cut these diagonally into 168 half-
square triangles.

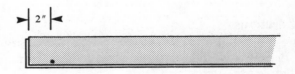

Main (B)

1. Cut 31 strips 1½″ wide. (Remember to
straighten your fabric frequently.)
2. Cut 7 strips 1½″ wide. Cut into 48 lengths
5½″ long.

3. Cut 5 strips 2″ wide.
4 Cut 4 strips 2″ wide. Cut into 48 segments
3½″ long.
5. (Peak) Cut 3 strips about ⅓₂″ less than 2¾″
wide. Open them up and make a stack of these 3
strips. Straighten left edge, then measure 2″ in
from top edge and make a dot.

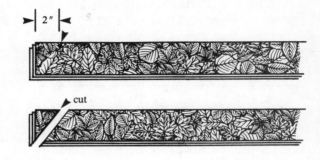

Cut from bottom left corner to dot.
    From these 2 starting points, measure off at
4″ intervals, then cut from dot to dot.

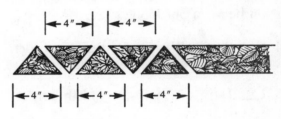

Cut 48 "peaks."
    6. Cut 9 strips 3½″ wide for last border.

For pieced border:

1. Cut 3 strips 5¼″ wide. Cut into 21 squares
5¼″. Then cut these with an X to yield 84 quarter-
square triangles.

2. Cut 6 strips 2″ wide.

Accent (C)

1. Cut 7 strips 2½″ wide. Make a stack of 4
strips and a stack of 3 strips (all right side up) and
straighten left edges. Measure in 2″ from bottom
and make a dot.

Cut from top edge to dot.

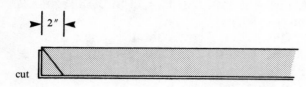

From these 2 starting points, measure off into 5⅝″ segments. Then cut from dot to dot.

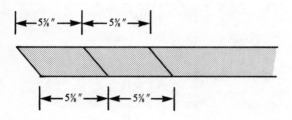

2. Cut 3 strips 2½″ wide. Cut into 35 squares 2½″ for lattice.

3. Cut 5 strips 2½″ wide for second border, which will be sewn onto long sides.

4. Cut 4 strips 2″ wide for second border, which will be sewn onto top and bottom.

5. Cut 9 strips 2″ wide for fourth border.

6. Cut 10 strips 2½″ wide for binding.

PIECING AND ASSEMBLY

This quilt can be pieced more efficiently if the house is broken down into 4 basic sections:

Chimney sections

Sew 2½ sets of strips that look like this:

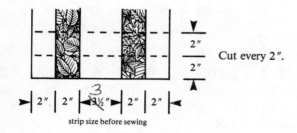

Roof sections

1. Sew a ⅞″ background strip to 1 side of parallelogram. Press and trim.

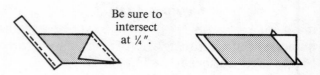

2. Add triangles of background fabric (A) to left side of peak and to right side of parallelogram. Sew units together.

Door section

1. Sew 6 sets of strips that look like this:

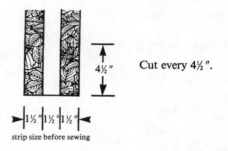

2. Add a 2″ by 3½″ main rectangle to tops.

3. Sew 1″ background strips to right sides.

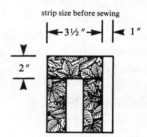

Window section

1. Sew 4 sets of strips that look like this:

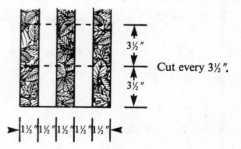

2. Sew a 1″ background (A) strip to each of 7 main (B) 1½″ wide strips. Press seams toward dark fabric. Cut into 48 segments 5½″ long. Sew to top of units made in step 1.

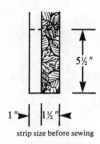

strip size before sewing

3. Add 5½″ strips of main fabric to bottom.

Piecing the House

1. Sew chimney section to top of roof section.
2. Sew door section to left side of window section.
3. Add roof/chimney sections to door/ window sections.

Setting the Quilt

1. Sew in 8 rows of 6 houses, with 9½″ lattice strips between houses.
2. Sew 9″ lattice strips with squares to form 7 strips that will go between rows.
3. Following illustration, assemble quilt.

Borders

1. For first border, piece 2″ wide background (A) strips (on the slant) and measure off 2 strips 61½″ long. Sew to top and bottom. Press.
   Measure off 2 strips 89½″ and sew these to long sides.
2. For second border, piece 2″ strips of accent fabric (C) (on the slant).
   Measure off 2 strips 64½″ and sew to top and bottom. Press.

3. Piece 2½″ strips of accent fabric (C) (on the slant). Measure off 2 strips 92½″ long and sew them to long sides. Press.

CREATIVE OPTION

After sewing on second border, you may add a pieced border.

1. Sew 6 sets of strips that look like this:

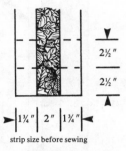

strip size before sewing

Cut every 2½″ into 84 segments.

2. Sew background triangles (A) onto each side of main (B) colored quarter-square triangles to make 84 Flying Geese units.

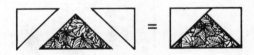

3. Sew each Flying Geese unit to 2½″ segments.

4. Sew 2 border strips of 17 arrows. Sew these to top and bottom of quilt, following illustration.
5. Sew 2 border strips of 25 arrows (notice the ends). Sew to long sides of quilt.
6. For fourth border, piece remaining 2″ strips of accent fabric (C) (on the slant). Measure off 2 strips 76½″ long and sew to top and bottom. Press.
   Measure off 2 strips 103½″ long and sew to long sides. Press.
7. Piece 3½″ wide main fabric (B) strips (on the slant) and measure off 2 strips 79½″ long. Sew to top and bottom. Press.
   Measure off 2 strips 109½″ long and sew to long sides. Press.

FEATHERED STAR QUILT

Recently, Feathered Star quilts have been the subject of renewed interest. I knew I had to make one, and I knew it had to be one that required no templates.

The cutting of a Feathered Star quilt seems endless due to the number of pieces, and the size of the pieces requires careful stitching, but the results are worth it. All who see this quilt are bound to be impressed. In my adaptation, I have also included a pieced border as a creative option. This quilt uses my techniques for bias mini-triangles, set-in piecing, and partial stitching. The tips given along the way should take the difficulty out of the piecing.

Lap Quilt

12 Feathered Star blocks, 11¼" finished
Pieced area finishes to 39¾" by 52½".
After first border, quilt will be 42" by 54".
After pieced border, quilt will be 45" by 57".
After last border, quilt will be 51" by 63".

Fabric A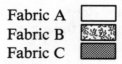
Fabric B
Fabric C

FABRIC REQUIREMENTS

Background (A)—3 yds. (2½ yds. for piecing, ½ yd. for pieced border)
Feather fabric (B)—2 yds. (1¼ yds. for piecing, ¾ yd. for last border)
Accent fabric (C)—2½ yds. (¾ yd. for piecing, ½ yd. for first border, ½ yd. for pieced border, ¾ yd. for binding)
Backing—4 yds.

CUTTING INSTRUCTIONS

Background (A)

1. Cut ½ yd. into 1½″ wide bias strips for mini-triangles (feathers).
2. Cut 5 strips 3⅞″ wide. Cut into 48 squares 3⅞″ for corners of stars.
3. Cut 2 strips 5⅞″ wide into 12 squares 5⅞″. Cut these squares with an X to yield 48 quarter-square triangles for sides of stars.

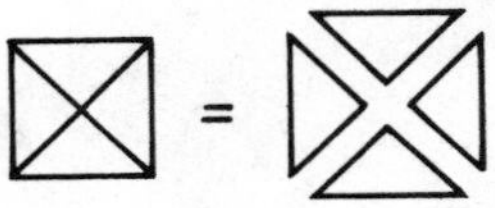

4. Cut 4 strips 1⅝″ wide. Cut into 96 squares 1⅝″. Cut these diagonally once to yield 192 loose half-square triangles.

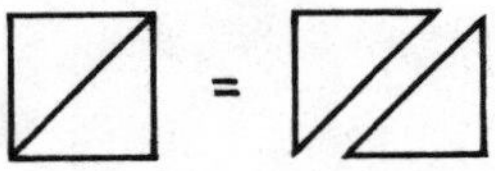

5. Cut 11 strips 2″ wide. Cut into 31 lengths of 11¾″ for lattice.

For pieced border:

Set aside ½ yd. to sew with accent fabric (C) for triangles.

Feather fabric (B)

1. Cut ½ yd. into 1½″ wide bias strips for mini-triangles (feathers).
2. Cut 3 strips 1¼″ wide. Cut into 96 squares 1¼″.
3. Cut 2 strips 3⅝″ wide. Cut into 12 squares 3⅝″ for centers of stars.
4. Cut 1 strip 2″ wide. Cut into 20 squares 2″ for lattice intersections.
5. Cut 7 strips 3½″ wide for last border.

Accent fabric (C)

1. Cut 6 strips 2⅛″ wide. Fold these strips in half, right sides together. Cut into 96 trapezoids, measuring cuts at 3⅛″ intervals. There will be 48 with their points going 1 way and 48 with points going opposite way. (See page 10 for more information on cutting trapezoids.)

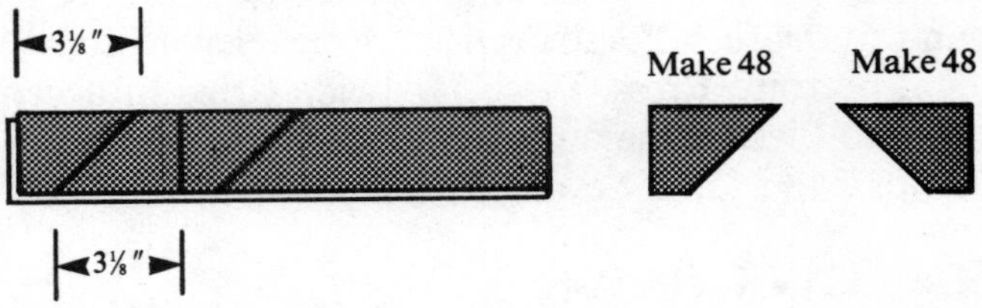

2. Cut 5 strips 1¼″ wide. Cut into 96 diamonds, measuring cuts at 1¼″ intervals.

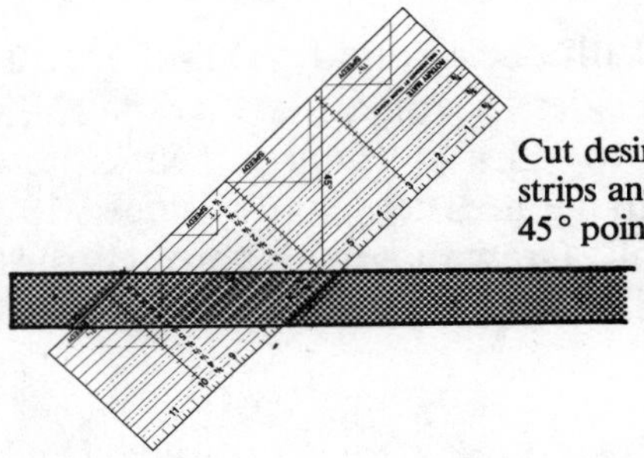

Cut desired width strips and cut a 45° point.

Make bias cuts every 1¼″, lining up 45-degree angle on ruler like this:

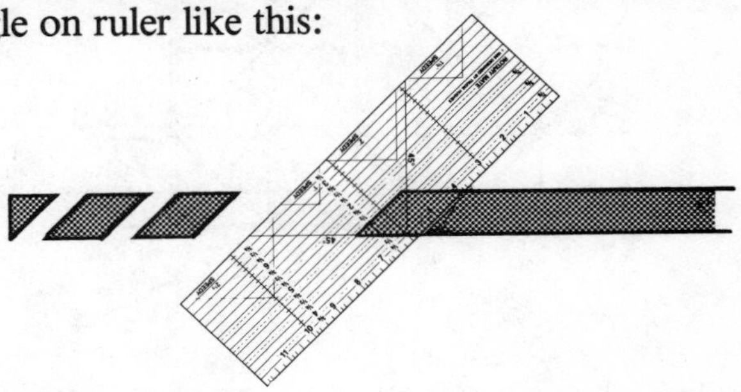

You should get 20 from each strip.

3. Cut 4 strips 1⅝″ wide for long sides of first border.
4. Cut 2 strips 1¼″ wide for short sides of first border.

5. Cut 7 strips 2½″ wide for binding.

For pieced border:

Set aside ½ yd. to sew with background fabric for triangles.

PIECING AND ASSEMBLY

1. Refer to directions given for large quilt on pages 93 and 94 to make 12 Feathered Star blocks.

2. Sew lattice strips (A) between blocks. Make 4 rows of 3 stars each. Sew lattice strips with 2″ squares of feather fabric (B) and sew these strips between rows.

3. Take 1¼″ wide strips of accent fabric (C) and measure off 2 strips 41¼″ long. Sew to top and bottom. Press. Piece 1⅛″ wide strips of accent fabric. Piece these on a slant and measure off 2 strips 54½″ long. Sew to long sides. Press.

CREATIVE OPTION

After first border, a pieced border may be added.

1. With background (A) and accent (C) fabrics right sides together, mark grids of 2⅜″. You will need to mark 66 squares. Mark these in sections to make it easier. You will need 132 triangle units in all. Draw diagonals through these squares to look like this:

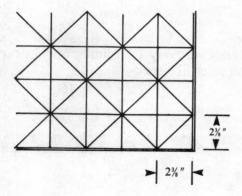

Stitch a ¼″ seam on each side of diagonal line. Cut apart and press.

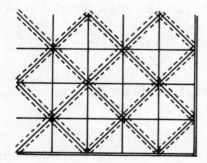

These should measure 2″ from raw edge to raw edge.

2. Make 2 strips of 28 triangles, reversing direction in the middle, to look like this:

Sew to top and bottom of quilt. Press.

3. Make 2 strips of 38 triangles, reversing direction in the middle, to look like this:

Sew to long sides of quilt. Press.

4. Piece 3½″ wide strips of feather fabric (B) (on the slant) and measure off 2 strips 45½″ long. Sew to top and bottom. Press. Measure off 2 strips 63½″ long and sew to long sides. Press.

Fabric A ☐   Fabric B ■   Fabric C ▨

Large Quilt

24 Feathered Star blocks, 11¼" finished
2¼" pieced sashing
Pieced area finishes to 56" by 83".
After first border, quilt will be 60" by 87".
After pieced borders, quilt will be 72" by 99".
After fifth border, quilt will be 75" by 102".
After last border, quilt will be 81" by 108".

FABRIC REQUIREMENTS

Background (A)—5½ yds. (3¼ yds. for piecing,
    2¼ yds. for pieced border)
Feather fabric (B)—6 yds. (2½ yds. for piecing,
    1¼ yds. for borders, 1 yd. for binding,
    1¼ yds. for pieced border)
Accent fabric (C)—3¾ yds. (2½ yds. for piecing,
    1¼ yds. for last border)
Backing—6½ yds.

CUTTING INSTRUCTIONS

Background (A)

1. Cut 2 half-yard pieces into 1½" wide bias strips for mini-triangles.

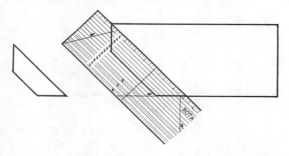

2. Cut 10 strips 3⅞" wide. Cut into 96 squares 3⅞" for corners of stars.
3. Cut 4 strips 5⅞" wide. Cut into 24 squares 5⅞". Cut these squares with an X to yield 96 quarter-square triangles for sides of stars.

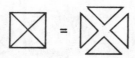

4. Cut 8 strips 1⅝" wide. Cut into 192 squares 1⅝". Cut these diagonally once to yield 384 loose triangles.

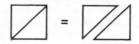

For pieced border:

1. Set aside 1¼ yds. to sew with feather fabric (B) for triangles.
2. Cut 9 strips 3½" wide.

Feather fabric (B)

1. Cut 2 half-yard pieces into 1½" wide bias strips for mini-triangles.
2. Cut 6 strips 1¼" wide. Cut into 192 squares 1¼".
3. Cut 3 strips 3⅜" wide. Cut these into 24 squares 3⅜" for centers of stars.
4. Cut 20 strips 1¼" wide for setting rails.
5. Cut 4 strips 1¼" wide for nine patches.
6. Cut 8 strips 2½" wide for first border.
7. Cut 9 strips 2" wide for fifth border.
8. Cut 10 strips 2½" wide for binding.

For pieced border:

1. Set aside 1¼ yds. to sew with background fabric (A) for triangles.
2. Cut 4 squares 2" for corners.

Accent fabric (C)

1. Cut 12 strips 2⅛" wide. Fold these strips in half, right sides together. Cut into 192 trapezoids, measuring cuts at 3⅛" intervals. There will be 96 with their points going 1 way and 96 with points going opposite way. (See page 10 for more information on cutting trapezoids.)

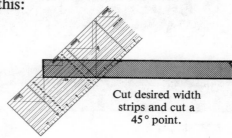

Make 96   Make 96

2. Cut 10 strips 1¼" wide. Cut into 192 diamonds, measuring cuts at 1¼". Layer 5 strips at a time. Using 45-degree line on ruler, make a cut like this:

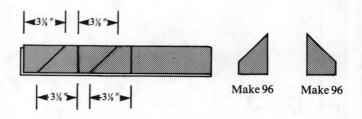

Cut desired width
strips and cut a
45° point.

Make bias cuts every 1¼", lining up 45-degree angle on ruler like this:

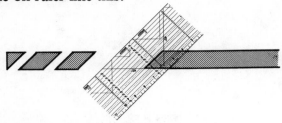

You should get 20 from 1 strip.

3. Cut 40 strips 1¼" wide to sew with feather fabric to make setting rails.
4. Cut 2 strips 1¼" wide for nine patches.
5. Cut 10 strips 3½" wide for last border.

PIECING AND ASSEMBLY

1. Sew bias strips of background (A) to feather fabric (B). Sew and press in pairs first. Sew 4 pairs together and press again. This amount should make enough triangles for several stars.

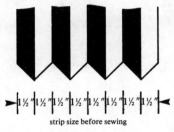

►|1½"|1½"|1½"|1½"|1½"|1½"|1½"|1½"|◄
strip size before sewing

Keeping 45-degree angle of ruler on a stitching line, make 1¼" bias cuts. (This cut puts you back on grain.)

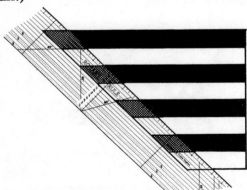

Starting at bottom, make straight cuts. Line up cross line of ruler with cut edge. Cut at each point along bottom edge.

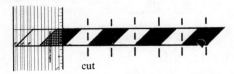

cut

Then starting back at left edge, measure off 1¼" and trim. This bit of extra trimming is a fudge factor I have built in to help make up for pressing and stitching errors you may have made. You now have perfect mini-triangles that form 1¼" cut squares, and these have already been pressed! For each block you will need 32 units that look like this:

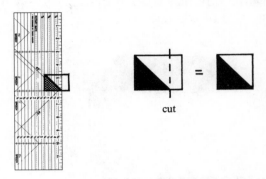

cut

2. Sew these mini-triangles in pairs. For each star, you will need 8 pairs going 1 direction and 8 pairs going opposite direction.

Make 8   Make 8

3. Sew a background triangle onto end of each pair.
Make sure that triangle is going same direction as other background triangles.

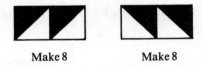

Make 8   Make 8

4. Add a small square of feather fabric (B) onto all combinations heading to the right to look like this:

Make 8

5. Take 4 pairs of each combination and add a diamond onto end.

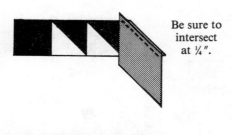

HINT: Make sure bias edge of diamond is sewn onto bias edge of triangle.

Be sure to intersect at ¼″.

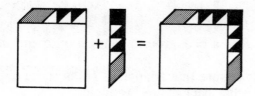

6. You will need 4 background squares for each star. Sew units with diamonds on ends to these squares.

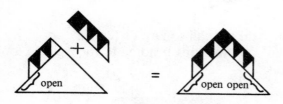

7. You will need 4 quarter-square triangles for each star. Sew remaining units onto triangles, ending stitching about 1 stitch past last seam.

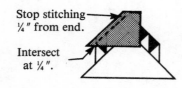

Sew 2 mirror-imaged trapezoids to these units. This piecing is very similar to doing an attic window. It is done with 3 separate seams.

Stop stitching ¼″ from end.

Intersect at ¼″.

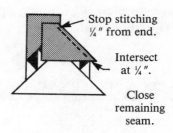

Stop stitching ¼″ from end.

Intersect at ¼″.

Close remaining seam.

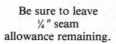

Be sure to leave ¼″ seam allowance remaining.

open open

8. Sew a corner unit onto each side of 2 of triangle units like this:

There will be 1 important intersection you will want to give attention to.

HINT: Use a pin to position the 2 intersections, then remove pin and place it to side. Don't panic; this intersection gets easier with each star.

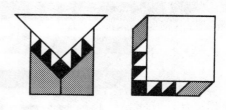

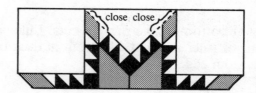

close close

Check this seam from front. If you are satisfied, close up remaining seam.

9. Sew remaining 2 triangle units to center square, then add 2 rows made in step 8.

Pieced Sashing

1. Sew 20 sets of strips that look like this:

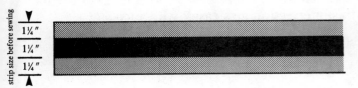

Cut into 11 lengths of 11¾". (Cut leftovers into 35 segments of 1¼" for row 2 of nine patches.) You will need 58 setting rails.

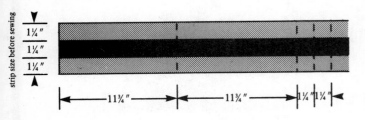

2. Make 3 sets of strips for nine patches that look like this:

Make 70 cuts at 1¼" intervals to make rows 1 and 3 of nine patches. Make 35 little nine patches that look like this:

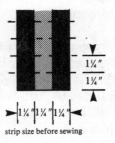

Sew 4 stars in each row. Separate with setting rails.

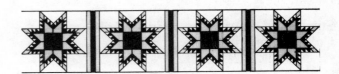

Sew 7 strips of setting rails, alternating with little nine patches. Join rows.

Borders

After pieced area is completed, add first border. Piece 2½" wide strips of feather fabric (B)(on the slant) and measure off 2 strips 56½" long. Sew to top and bottom. Press.

Measure off 2 border strips 87½" long and sew to long sides. Press.

CREATIVE OPTION

After first border, you can add a pieced border to add more interest.

1. With background (A) and feather fabric (B) right sides together, mark grids of 2⅜". You will need to mark 210 squares. Mark these in sections to make it easier. You will need 420 triangle units in all. Draw diagonal lines through squares to look like this:

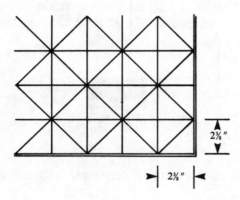

Stitch a ¼" seam on both sides of diagonal line. Cut apart and press.

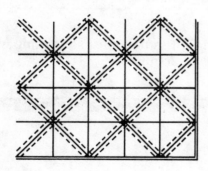

These should measure 2" from raw edge to raw edge.

← 2" →

2. Sew 2 strips of 40 triangles, reversing direction in the middle, referring to large diagram on page 91 for complete segment. Stitch to top and bottom. Press.

3. Sew 2 strips of 60 triangles, reversing direction in the middle, referring to large diagram on page 91 for complete segment. Stitch to long sides. Press.

4. Piece 3½" wide strips of background fabric (A) (on the slant) and measure off 2 strips 63½" long. Sew to top and bottom. Press.
   Measure off 2 strips 96½" long and sew to long sides of quilt. Press.

5. Sew 2 strips of 46 triangles, reversing direction in the middle. Stitch to top and bottom. Press.

6. Sew 2 strips of 64 triangles, reversing direction in the middle. Add a square of feather fabric (B) to each end and stitch to sides of quilt.

7. Piece 2" wide strips of feather fabric (B) (on the slant) and measure off 2 strips 72½" long. Sew to top and bottom of quilt. Press. Measure off 2 strips 102" long and sew to long sides of quilt. Press.

8. Piece 3½" wide strips of accent fabric (C) (on the slant) and measure off 2 strips 75½" long. Sew to top and bottom. Measure off 2 strips 108½" and sew to long sides. Press.